P|

G000154810

"I was ashamed of myself
costume party; and I atte
- Franz

Neurodiversity refers to the concept that neurological
differences, such as autism, ADHD, or dyslexia,
should be recognized and respected as part of
natural human diversity. It promotes the idea that
these differences are not disorders or deficits, but
rather unique variations of the human brain.
We hope to have covered most of the 'labels' under
the umbrella of 'neurodiversity'.

~~~~~~~~~~~~~~~~~~~~~~~~~~~~~~~~~~~~~~

Section	Author	Title
Interlude 1	Gali Rosas	
Foreword	Dr James Leong	
Introduction	Carolyn Street	
Chapter 1	Steven Alexander Simmonds	Neurodiversity And Me
Chapter 2	Gemma Sandwell	Positive Psychology and Neurodiversity
Chapter 3	Didi Kan	We Are All The Continuation Of A Story
Interlude 2	Roy Payamal	
Interlude 3	Mamie Philp	Each One of You Unique
Chapter 4	Tal Stein	Positives Out Of Negatives
Chapter 5	Noor Ashikin Binte Shahirudin	Self-Care, A Social Life And Self-Development
Chapter 6	Mandy Street	Autistic Thoughts
Chapter 7	Carolyn Street	Navel Gazing For A Good Cause
Chapter 8	Carolyn Street	My Experiences And Inperiences
Chapter 9	Becky Hart	My Journey
Interlude 4	Stephanie Fam	Cuddling
Inerlude 5	DJ Robinson	Celebrating Neurodiversity Welcome to my Normal

Interlude One

By Gali Rosas

It says: "Everyone Is Good At Something…. Let's
Help Each Other"

Midnightmommymoments.blogspot.com
Gali Rosas can also be reached on Facebook,
Instagram and by snail mail to the publisher:)

Foreword

By Dr James Leong

You are about to embark on a journey of discovery that will change your life and the lives of those around you. You are about to enter the world of neurodiversity, a term that may be new to you but is essential to understand in our diverse world. Neurodiversity refers to the natural variation in how people think and learn. It encompasses conditions such as ADHD, dyslexia, dyspraxia and autism, which are not deficits but differences. Everyone is unique and has something to offer.

As a Master NLP Trainer and Hypnotherapy Teacher who has trained psychologists, counselors and psychiatrists, I have seen the power and potential of neurodiverse people. I have also seen the challenges and struggles they face in a world that is not always designed for them. I have realized that there is a lot of room for growth and learning when talking to my peers and the general public.

I have always been fascinated by the human mind and how it works. I have also been curious about the different ways people perceive and interact with the world. I have met many amazing people who have taught me valuable lessons about life, creativity, and resilience. Some of them have been diagnosed with neurodiverse conditions, and some of them have not. But they all have one thing in common: they are beautiful and brilliant in their own way.

In this book, you will learn more about neurodiversity and how it affects people's lives. You will discover the benefits and talents of neurodiverse people, as well as the challenges they face in a world that is not always designed for them. You will also learn how to create a more inclusive and supportive workplace culture for everyone. You will find practical tips and tools to help you observe, listen and create a safe environment for others to ask and receive support. You will also learn how to educate yourself and others about neurodiversity and how to be curious, compassionate, supportive and patient.

In addition, you will find chapters on modalities to help neurodiverse clients in the healing industry. You will learn how to explore their identities, labels, diagnosis, beliefs, strengths, fears, concerns, and challenges. You will learn how to help them go from shame to pride in who they are. You will also find inspiring stories of how others have triumphed over their mental illnesses with the help of neurodiversity coaching.

I hope this book will open your eyes to the beauty of neurodiversity and inspire you to celebrate the gift of diversity in yourself and others. Neurodiversity is not only crucial for the human race but also for each individual's happiness and fulfillment.

Thank you for reading this book and joining me on this journey of discovery. You are about to discover a new way of seeing yourself and others, a new way of living with joy and purpose, a new way of being human.

Dr James Leong's Bio

Dr. James Leong is a visionary leader who ignites the potential of executives to overcome their traumas and achieve breakthrough results with his cutting-edge expertise in Neuroscience, NLP, Gestalt Therapy, Ericksonian Hypnotherapy, and the Enneagram. He is a trailblazer and a game-changer who leads the way in the field of Neuroscience and Executive Coaching, and his work has inspired and transformed the lives of many individuals. Dr. James is also a captivating speaker who shares his insights and wisdom at international conferences and workshops, where he always leaves a lasting impact.

Dr James Leong is a / an:
Accredited Teacher of the Enneagram
Master NLP Trainer (NLP University)
Hypnosis Teacher and Organization Member of Accredited Counsellors, Coaches, Psychotherapists and Hypnotherapists (ACCPH, UK)
Professional Certified Coach (ICF)
Chartered Management Consultant
James@jamesleong.com
James's website is at www.jamesleong.com
https://instagram.com/drjamesleong?igshid=ZDc4OD BmNjlmNQ==

Introduction
By Carolyn Street

Dear Reader,

With that fantastic foreword setting the tone for our book, here is the introduction by me, Carolyn. I call myself the compiler but I like to think of myself as the casting department, the director, the producer and the one that gets the equivalent of an Oscar for the final product.

Formatting, bringing the contents from disparate files to a book-book both e-book and paperback is the biggest job including uploading to Amazon is all credit to Snigdha Bhowmik who deserves a medal.

At the end of the book is a work in progress that explains the ins and outs, vision, mission and purpose and an overview of what it is all about; White Paper on the 'And Us' Series.

A sincerely happy, hearty and warm welcome to this curated collection of stories and sharings all to do with how we the authors have encountered and gone about handling Neurodiversity in many of its forms. We hope that you find resonance and encouragement as well as useful insights into how you or your dear ones and peers or clients can adopt or adapt the contents for when things get a bit much.

This book is designed for you to read at your own pace and leisure. We are most mindful that we are here with rich, substantial content on neurodiversity, a subject on which there is so much input available. But the input is not reflective of our personal experiences. We are familiar with the 'you are not..'s, 'you don't…'s and 'why can't you…'s from those that label us. We also in turn adopt those labels like 'autistic', 'hyperactive' 'inattentive' with strange and weird behaviours. Not to mention 'disorganised' 'unmotivated' and not 'normal'. I will leave the discussion of what 'normal' is for another occasion.

We admire Stephen Wiltshire* who is 'autistic' but can draw entire cityscapes in minute detail from a single view from a helicopter. He picked up a pencil one day and his abilities were unlocked. Many of us do not know what our gifts and skills are as we never had the chance to try out the activities we may excel in.

And there is so much stigma. And so many well-meaning coaches, TikTokers, Instagram reelers and the like who have tips. The internet is overwhelming and these platforms force you to see content that may be triggering before you can select your content maker of choice.

We choose to share our offerings in a book as it can be hard to know which set of tips on social media and so on - are suitable for us.

As the saying goes 'to assume is to make an ass of you and me'. But people - in my point of view - who aim to fit us into neat boxes are the xxxxs. I say that while not wanting to insult asses… That reminds me, putting my editor's hat back on, that I have only edited the chapters for punctuation and spelling and clarity. Unlike all the other 'And Us' books I have not attempted to place constraints on the authors such as imposing a style guide or stipulating English spellings. I daresay I speak for most of us when I say 'that's not us'. If anything about the layout triggers you, that's an interesting point of view (an Access

Conscious phrase which is immensely useful when we have unpleasant reactions or find ourselves tut-tutting or judging things). I firmly believe that what we like in others is the traits we wish we had or traits we already have. What we dislike or tut-tut about are traits we secretly wish we could have.

'What do you mean?' - a retort I dread but know is coming whenever I attempt to explain something about my 'condition' which to me may be self-explanatory yet I find myself explaining 'what it says on the tin'. For me we are the ones with the attention. Ooh controversial. Forgive me, I just overshared. No offence meant (out comes my fawning / people-appeasing or pleasing response because I am afraid that Neurotypicals reading this might get offended). Here, my tongue is 'firmly in cheek'. Cheekiness is a great strategy in my view.

The contributors to this compilation were personally invited to share their valuable experiences, expertise and guidance whether received or gained by our own learnings. We have our unique viewpoints and hope that each chapter has something for everyone.

We are a diverse group, as one would expect. There is no 'lead chapter' as we are all unique and have value of our own as a collective and as individuals. The chapters are grouped as such: coaches and therapists first (except me), then the parents, then me then the experienced experts, all of whom could easily be counselors, confidants and/ or therapists.

While our place of origin, ethnicity, lineage, colour creed and credentials are equally respectable, credible and sincere, it is the norm to provide some information on who is from where and our backgrounds. Each chapter comes with a bio of the writer and we hope you will contact those of us you resonate with the most.

Some of us are Singaporeans; we hail from the 'Tiny Red Dot' here in the Tropics.

Dr James Leong, my Master Neurolinguistic Programmiing trainer and 'Sifu', or teacher in Chinese. His foreword was a real score for me, being someone I trust to have the empathy and expertise to do justice to the role.

Clement, Jireh, Ze Shi, Shikin and my husband Rennie and I are Singaporeans and based here. I am categorised as 'English' in terms of race due to the patriarchical approach in operation. I do get responses of 'but you are not Chinese, how can you be Singaporean?' also 'you don't speak like a Singaporean'. But I digress. We have kept our chapters secular in tone except when it would be inauthentic not to.

Roy, a dear friend and one of the very few buskers and artists in Singapore, is a varied talent who inspires enormously as he is simply himself. His perspectives are works of art. His interlude (shorter freeform piece) epitomises natural creativity and new paradigms of interpreting the world around us. This also goes for Stephanie, an established poet, writer and decorated speaker. She is not neurodiverse in the classic sense of the word but her perspectives, as someone with physical disabilities, have a unique, fascinating and also attractive quality to them. Her interludes are drawings and inspiring as they show us that art is what you make it.

Arunditha Emmanuel shows an oft-sidelined exposé of vulnerability and truth in her poem 'Day'.

We also have an anonymous interlude by a regular contributor as a bonus.

Mandy, Tal, Gemma, Didi, Becky and Steven are all in various parts of England as is Gudrun, my go-to Shamanic healer and mutual mentor. Mamie is in the UK too from my top 5 favourite city Edinburgh in Scotland. Her interlude is a gem, she being a teacher with a heart for those with diverse needs. And not.

We have two interludes by DJ Robinson, who hails from Syracuse in the US. A poem on what her life has been like with her brand of autism and a piece on the uniqueness and intelligence of her older grandson. Gali's interlude is one of her sharings I pinched from Facebook. She too is an indespensible breeze chivvying this project along.

As the curator, compiler, editor and publisher of this series I am extremely chuffed to say that I know all the authors personally. Some are close friends and others I have come to admire and be inspired by over social media and their online presences.

In alphabetical order, here are small abstracts, one for each chapter.

Becky writes in 'My Journey' about her life and shares her personal experiences in a lovely piece that is generous in its invitation to the reader to come and discover what she has to share. Labels are really inconsequential, being imposed by the external world. Thank you Becky for accepting the invitation and for sharing. And my eternal thanks to Tal for introducing us. Becky helped me hugely with an

13

admin task, being in the UK she was instrumental in getting some copies of 'And Us' book 7, 'Grief & Us' to me here in Singapore. Her help was invaluable. One thing led to the next and here we have a chapter that is both engaging and relatable with a sincerity and voice that are really enjoyable and uplifting.

Carolyn ah me... chapter seven is a selection of my real-life client stories. I am a therapist with several clients 'on the spectrum' and not. My labels (who would have them except they help with languaging) are ADH'd' diagnosed at 50 and a half but suspected since I started exploring the whats and whys and wherefores of being on this planet as me. (Will explain the little d, honest). I also have self-identified dyspraxia aka clumsy Carolyn syndrome. If I had a dollar for every time I have tripped up the stairs... LOL. Failed at stacking shelves at a well-known convenience store as well as counting money (of course). I share these so people who feel that therapy is not for them may know that there are safe spaces. There is understanding and sameness or at least understanding. More in my / our respective bios of course.

Chapter eight is a sharing of my own experiences with the abovementioned 'labels' and other peculiarities. Also, as a therapist, coach and trainer with impressive Executive Function Disorder (under ADHD) as well as 20 years of functioning as a lecturer and my practice as a psychotherapist and energy therapist under my belt. Not to blow my own trumpet; I gained insights from the various modalities I undertook certification in that helped me understand my foibles and my challenges and the way I see the world. And that led to this, the
'And Us' series. More in the chapter, including the down-, up- and farsides. My sense of humour saves

my bacon and I hold on to the saying 'There is no failure, only feedback' for dear life.

Oh and if some of the labels are unfamiliar, fret not. We have a glossary of terms for reference.

Clement's chapter, entitled 'Limbo', is highly insightful, interesting and engaging look at his experiences as someone diagnosed with 'Non-verbal learning disorder'.

The chapter on crystals opened up an opportunity for us to explore how we view and apply these gifts from the earth as helpers with our task management, self-esteem, confidence and as part of our individual repertoires of resources to aid us in managing our various challenges. As it turns out we all use them but as is the case with secret recipes, some are loath to share their go-tos in case they 'don't work' for others. And indeed, how we interact with crystals is both personal and changeable over time. Louise Romaniuk inspired the chapter and provided most of the key information which aligned or was new to what I had empirically observed or experienced. Thanks Louise, a wonderful uplifting online friend and fellow coach.

Didi shares with us his view of the world as someone with a blend of labels and foibles. He has taken on innumerable challenges and emerged as someone with a strength and vision and mission that inspires me and those around him. He is another of my go-to therapists of choice. As the one writer who has been part of all the 'And Us' books with me, also a therapist of Rapid Transformational Therapy, he is the voice of consistency in the series.

Gemma is another dear esteemed friend and incredible coach and therapist. As with many of the others she is one of my go-to therapists of choice. Her chapter on Positive Psychology is another truly refreshing one. She raises and updates awareness of 'Highly Sensitive People', Positive Resilience and the hugely important topic of boundaries.

I love Jireh's chapter 'The Hero With a Thousand Masks' - A Journey to Integration' because it is by him (needless to say, the same goes for all the authors lol). For real, he has orchestrated it like a maestro. He lends insight and vulnerability to a mega-chapter with multifarious approaches and facets. As someone with autism and Attention Deficit Hyperactivity Disorder, his perspectives enrich and entertain and cannot help to educate. For the first time I have a chapter that is longer than the set limit of five thousand words. I have not split it up as it is a cohesive whole.

Mandy's chapter is another godsend. She shares her own experiences as a field expert and those of a parent of two amazing daughters on the spectrum. I love the way she says: (I identify) 'as 'late-identified autistic woman and neurodivergent-affirming specialist clinician'. Delicious :)

Norashikin, Shikin for short, is someone who has really been resilient and truly inspiring in that she took action and really optimised her situation as the mum of a son on the spectrum. She shares how self-care and self-development have not only been coping strategies but edifying, enriching and her every word is well-worth the read.

Selective Mutism was written by me from my point of view without my points of view; if that makes sense. I held my proverbial tongue. Well, as you'll see I did indulge in a little dramatic hyperbole for effect. But it is all the truth. It is on behalf of Steven Rennie Johns, my spouse who sees no need to talk and communicate the majority of the time. His whole life he was shut down, shut out and consequently, shut himself in. To me, he, as a Heyoka empath, sees the higher order (in his perspective) to things. He believes he is not good enough and neither is anything he has to say. The 'selective' in 'selective mute' is a fascinating phenomenon for all, and a conundrum for me, his talkaholic wife. But that is too much information and not the angle of this collection. I crowdsourced a section from people who work with the 'disorder' and therapists.

Steven Alexander's is a gentle, realistic and raw view of different facets of Neurodiversity. His discussion of anxiety and how it underpins so many of the ND experiences is truly authentic, real and immediately 'getable'. His sharings are a wonderful mix of personal and interactive insights.

Tal has a view of parenting and relating to one's child that lifts and dispels any negativity surrounding the role of a parent of a child on the spectrum. Given the choices Tal has made about the direction she wanted her professional life to take since her son received his diagnosis, she now firmly believes she knows the answer to the question she asked herself at the time, "why me?" Because she is determined to be one of the individuals who encourages employers to reconsider their perceptions of how much neurodiverse people can achieve. Her son, Becky and the young people she is helping find paid work in her current job, are the people who prove her point. In her own (and her mother's) words, she's found the reason she's on this planet!

Ze Shi has a way with words which has me hooked. He uses a musical metaphor 'The Wrong Note' to portray his theme as someone who has learnt a lot the hard way. It would be cliched to say we have all been through the School of Hard Knocks and come out to share the tale. But I just did. LOL.

It is our wish that in the pages that follow, you will find abundant food for thought and many interesting and even edifying sections.

Who this book is for: we have three main groups of people we do this work for. First and foremost for readers who picked up this book hoping for ideas, support, solidarity, how-tos, understanding and an empathetic source of help from experts and non-experts alike. Please please use this as a sort of inroads into the sorts of approaches and stories we the authors love and found invaluable. Do not hesitate to reach out. Seek professional support, please. We are here to complement medicine not replace it. We do not discuss medicines nor any form of homeopathics or any orally-administered substances because that would be beyond our purview and scope.

For readers who aim to gain an understanding of the elements and ins and outs of neurodiversity because a loved one is going through neurodiversity, you are one of the key audience-groups for our work. Thank you. The same goes for professionals who have the desire to help but have not got the life experiences; where knowledge may be theoretical, academic or third-hand or hearsay / through case-studies. Sorry to say compassion and true understanding cannot be acquired from anything but lived experiences; and the science backs that up. An exception is some threads of research that say it is all in the mind. But where did they expect it to be?

Neurodiversity and Us is the eighth book in the 'And Us' series; find out more in the free Facebook group 'Life Issues Transformed And Us' which you are most welcome to join as a reader of this book.

A quick word on what this book is not - it is anything but the sort of 'x number of infallible / Shut Up and Move On (a book with that title exists and it is brilliant; I am just using that phrase here for illustration) guaranteed steps to sort out your neurodiversity or be a definitive guide. Worse still 'x proven strategies to overcome your struggle with y condition'. I have had numerous clients who have, in their enthusiasm and naivete, done programmes like 'Guerilla this' 'that bootcamp' not to mention 'Unleash the other'; only to be at best out of pocket and regretful and at worst beaten down, broken, stripped of what self-esteem they had, and out of pocket. God bless you Zam. I speak as a former self-help junkie, so I'm a fine one to talk. Anyway…

One size cannot fit many, let alone all.
We all have one thing in common - a spirit of 'sharing is caring' and a desire to facilitate healing, learning and recovery for the benefit of our readership. As the saying goes, a (solved) problem shared is a problem halved - though that only happens when one has truly emerged from the trauma and lived to tell the tale.

Some of the chapters and interludes feature content and experiences which might be overwhelming or intense to some; a feature of the rawness and realness of the narratives all of which come with solutions and learnings that are invaluable takeaways.

A word about our logo, affectionately called 'The Jellyfish' purely due to its resemblance to the marine creatures. To me, it shows emotions, states of mind, heart and spirit bubbling up, up and away with the angels or down and through to Mother Earth who can transmute anything. (On the books and name cards it's exit stage left or right). Hence the colours of the book covers. Tangerine was the colour of choice for this volume as it is in the 'orange' family but has its own special something. An X factor, if you like (we do).

Please contact us without hesitation at the email addresses or social media messenger platforms listed in our bios. Join the Facebook group for content that is not shared in this volume like our live videos and shared online content.

We all wish you growth, peace and excitement in a conducive balance that suits you, emergence and wholeness.

Carolyn and the Neurodiversity And Us Team
    Singapore
    July, 2023
Ref: https://www.stephenwiltshire.co.uk/index.aspx is Stephen Wiltshire's website.

Steven's Bio

Steven Alexander is an experienced life coach in the U.K with over 20 years' experience of working in the community and urban areas with high levels of crime, poverty and deprivation.

Dedicating his life to "love and serve" Steven Alexander has a huge heart for those struggling with life, relationships, work and need that extra support.

Steven offers budgeting, counseling, mentoring, mediation, hypnotherapy, and Neuro Linguistic programming locally, nationally, and internationally.

A lover of nature, Steven can often be found walking along the beach, rivers, and places of tranquillity.

Steven brings a lot of fun, laughter, energy, and smiles wherever he goes seeking to share what he describes as "life in all its fullness."

LinkedIn: www.linkedin.com/in/steven-alexander-simmonds

His TikTok is @stevenalexandersimmonds

Radio link: www.facebook.com/ThisisThriveUK

Threads: Stevenalexandersimmonds

Chapter One

Neurodiversity And Me

By Steven Alexander Simmonds

"Stupid"
"Odd"
"Trouble"
"Dreamer"
Familiar words to so many.

Words such as these still haunt me to this day, plus many others said from those around me back in the day growing up. For those with any neurodiversity traits, it appears that many shares similar experiences of being called or labelled as such. These words can be emotionally damaging to those who are extra sensitive, and can be carried around for a lifetime.

Autism, was barely known about, heard of or spoken about back in the 80's 90's.

Some of the "naughty" kids had the label of "ADHD" whatever that meant back then, but "neurodiversity" as it is known now, not at all! Those children were often ridiculed and ostracised, almost treated as though they had a disease by their peers.

My name is Steven Alexander, and I have been helping and supporting people for over twenty years. I have two children, and work in the healthcare sector.

I offer on line support as well as one to one meet ups. I studied, counselling, sociology, psychology, hypnotherapy, neuro- linguistic programming as a way of trying to understand others more as well as myself. Struggling with mental health for many years, as well as life in general, I began to study personal development.

Personal development taught me many things including confidence, self-esteem and assertiveness.

Growing up, I had what is now "obvious autistic traits" however, I was not diagnosed until an adult, out of pure self-discovery and a need to know why I behaved in a certain way.

Welcome to this chapter!

I aim to take you not only my own personal journey, but also share with your professional tricks that many of us use both personally and in our line of work.

Anxiety

Ever suffer with anxiety?

After a life time of living with anxiety, it seems only right I start with this. Anxiety can be really debilitating, and can stunt quality of life. It is my personal mission to help those who suffer with anxiety.

"Breathe"

"Just breathe"

These were the wise words of a friend of mine as they listened to me recently. I share them with you, because one day this mantra, may come in useful, or save your life!

"Breathe!"

Often, we take breathing for granted, and seems an odd thing to begin a chapter with, yet helping people with breathing, is just one tool we use when supporting people with anxiety.

When we become anxious, often, our breathing can become heavier, quicker, we can hyper ventilate, and we can lose touch with reality, logic and rationalism.

Breathing techniques, can help to self-regulate the mind, and re-stabilise the chemical imbalance.

Anxiety is a huge topic in itself, and just because you have anxiety, it does not necessarily mean you are neurodivergent, nor does being neurodivergent mean you will suffer with anxiety.

Anxiety treatment can include anything from medication to therapy. Not all medication is suitable for everyone, and similarly not all therapies will work on all. Sometimes it is possible to find the root of the issue, and then help can be given accordingly, other times it can take a variety of different solutions and some anxieties are trauma based.

Post Traumatic Stress Disorder, is becoming more commonly recognised, diagnosed and talked about, and thankfully there is help available.

The work I do as a coach, can often include helping people with trauma and anxiety.

What is Neurodivergence?

Neurodivergence, is still a relatively new concept as a term, however many of the conditions linked with neurodiversity have been around for many years. It was not until as recent as 1998, when Judy Singer, an Australian sociologist, coined the word "neurodiversity" in recognition that everyone's brain develops differently.

Many people may have a condition. but yet undiagnosed, and some may even have a misdiagnosis. as there can be so many overlaps.

There is a huge gap of provision, sadly, between the support available to those with a formal diagnosis, and those without, certainly in regards to funding or extra support in the education system, and possibly working environment.

Access to support can be costly and timely, however there is help out there, and knowing who and where to get that support from, can be a mental battle in itself, but do not give in!

There is free and low-cost support out there too, so help, does not have to be costly, but worth the investment. Good help is often hard to find, however there are many support groups and individuals out there that may be worth networking with for additional support.

Often friends, family, partners, may not always be the best people to go to for help, and this can be frustrating, however, patience and understanding is better when it is reciprocal. I will cover relationships, later on in the chapter.

Common Traits of Autism and ADHD

There are many strands of autism, and the spectrum is wide. In this chapter I will unpack a little of my own experiences.

Attention Span - Being able to focus or hold attention for long periods of time can be hard without disappearing off into a dream space.

Focus can be very tricky with a tendency towards distractions, putting things off, or procrastinate.

*Patience is required

*Reinforce priorities and why things need to be done.

*Overwhelm can sometimes be a barrier, so smaller tasks are better.

*Encouragement rewards and incentives work better than any punishment

Behaviours - Sometimes behaviour, mood, emotions can be erratic. The more the mind is chaotic, the more extreme behaviours can be, or the person may become withdrawn. Sometimes this is linked to a chemical imbalance in the head or body, other times, other factors may be at play such as anxiety and overwhelm or frustrations.

Medication may be a source of help, so consulting medical advice is important, other times, the behaviour could be trying to communicate that the person is struggling.

Look out for inconsistencies of behaviour, or what may appear as" out of character" behaviour. These are key signs that something is wrong. On these occasions "what is wrong" may not help, however offering assurance, attentiveness, love and care, will often work better.

Often on these occasions the person trying to help may make assumptions, offer advice, may make judgements but these may be better being avoided to prevent further unravelling or what may be perceived as challenging behaviours. Some actions may back fire or escalate things. Space, empathy, understanding are much better allies.

Communication - There are many forms of communication. An understanding of different models is beneficial to both those with neurodiversity, but also for those trying to communicate with someone who is neurodivergent. Top Tip: Research communication styles!

There may be some ways that work a lot better than others.

A lot of people with neurodiversity can struggle with communication but may not have the confidence to share this, or have the skill set or awareness to teach someone how best to understand them. Top Tip: Research learning styles

Sensory Issues - Not everyone suffers with sensory issues, and those that do will differ greatly from one another. Loud noises, high pitched, vibrations of music, passing traffic, fan noises, tv volumes, sound of electricity flowing, lots of people talking, a room full of lots of different noises are just examples. These noises can make us either hold our ears, some might cry, scream, and the feeling is extremely unsettling. Sound issues can be managed through equipment such as noise reducing earphones, moving away from noisy environments, or trying to reduce the noises where possible.

Certain hair-dryers in public places can make me have this scream effect, and in work places, it can often be difficult to manage. It is always advisable to let work or your educational establishment or those around you aware of your sensory needs.

Lighting, or rather too much unnatural light can be overbearing for me, so I prefer dim lights or even darkness at times. Again, lighting is an issue for some.

While this may come under the section of relationships, often touching, hugs, holding hands, intimacy can be a struggle for some. This can be very hard emotionally for friends, family, partners, loved ones.

Somebody with sensory issues may not always be fully aware of what is wrong or be able to communicate as such, but look out for behaviour changes, or any spiraling of behaviour.

Truthfully, it is possible to write books around this subject alone, as it can be both simple and complex. Taking the time to find out more, and investigate further is a great investment.

Social interactions - Personally, for me, these have been a struggle. I prefer small gatherings to a large one, I hate crowds, waiting in lines agitate me, speaking to people can be very hard because of taking in what they are saying without distractions.

Many people with neurodiversity are great mimickers of others in order to try and fit in better, or hide any insecurities or their disability.

This mimicking can become an art form, a great skill set and extremely useful. Often those around may not be aware this is happening, as us humans, like those who are like ourselves. We can feel comfortable around such people, and even any differences are often accepted, over looked or less questioned.

Relationships - This topic gives me overwhelm just thinking about this, which says something in itself about the complexity and depth we could go here. Relationships in general can be difficult for the best of us, and maybe this is a lack of role modelling, teaching, education around this subject, the complexity of us as humans, the list is endless.

There are resources available to help all of us obtain better relationships such as books, courses, therapy, coaching is all available as well as support groups, on-line videos, internet etc.

Relationships take time, commitment, effort, patience, empathy, but for some with neurodiversity, relationships can be harder because of the levels of energy required and self-regulation to maintain them as well as themselves. Many of us have things going on mentally, so the additional mental strain relationships can bring can be just too much for many of us.

Time management - The rabbit in the story of Alice in Wonderland was known for his catchphrase of "I'm late, I'm late" Similarly time management can be an issue for some because of their neurodiversity. This can be for many reasons, but may include things like;

- Not prioritising tasks
- Distractions, day dreaming (lack of focus)
-Lethargy (lack of energy so things take longer)

Rest - Those with neurodiversity struggle to rest until they crash. Stopping still, resting, can seem quite alien and uncomfortable due to the level of mental energy in their head, making it hard to just stop, or find enough peace to enjoy that moment of rest. Tell someone to rest and this although maybe beneficial to that person from one perspective, can actually create huge levels of agitation and anxiety. In their mind they can then feel confined, restricted, almost punished, causing high levels of stress. We are "doing" people, often have to be "fiddling" with something or can appear literally restless. While ADHD folk are renowned for their high levels of energy, what many do not see. is the inability to switch off or the "crashing" which can take a good while to recover from.

Rest is still vitally important, so finding down time which works is hugely beneficial. This might be trial and error. For me, personally, walking is a very restful activity as it requires very little mental energy and a good way to burn off any excess energy. Walking offers a sense of freedom away from the normal demands and constraints of life. I was once offered a book on "How to find rest" however the mental energy required to read it was often too much.

Meditations are a great resource of help. Simple things such as playing rain sounds, sea sounds, nature, are ways of helping to calm and soothe the brain. A good thing about mediation is that there are so many ways to engage now, and something that I use myself a lot and I help others to use too.

Money Matters - Like everything in life, there are those good with it, and those who are just not. It is not correct to say that all neurodivergent people struggle financially however I can empathise with those who struggle. There are many reasons why so many struggle, and support should be done on an individual basis, however common traits can come into play such as struggling to manage priorities communicating with those who they owe debts to, health issues can prevent or reduce the ability to earn, and overwhelm as well as anxiety panics people. Due to social anxiety and speaking to others, asking for help can be a nightmare, so people struggle more.

There is no shame in asking for help, but I understand why many do not. Having an understanding and an awareness myself, means I am able to help in so many ways.

Snap shot

This chapter is really only the tip of the iceberg, perhaps not even that, however for those seeking help, or a greater awareness, it offers some insight into subjects that are often not talked about enough.

Further and more in-depth support is given to those I support and build relationships with, but I encourage everyone to study personal development in order to understand themselves more and those around them.

Peace be with you.

Steven Alexander Simmonds

Gemma's Bio

Gemma Sandwell is an Energy Alignment Coach for Leaders of the New Paradigm who are making a difference using their sensitivities as superpowers.

She is passionate about using Positive Psychology and the Quantum to become authentic and flourishing

Gemma has used all the extensive knowledge from being a Leadership Coach and Mindfulness Lead in a Blue-Chip company, studying Positive Psychology, Mindfulness, Coaching, Energy and the Quantum and doing a TEDx to create her courses and programmes.

Gemma has helped hundreds of Leaders and Entrepreneurs to increase their income and impact on the world by using their sensitivities as superpowers and getting in touch with their most Authentic Selves.

Her purpose is to enable you to tap into your own potential, connect with your authentic self and superpower strengths and create the business and life of your dreams. Gemma Sandwell Bsc Hons, Dip.PP, ICF ACC True Quantum Healer

Gemma's website is:
https://www.gemmasandwell.com

Chapter Two

Positive Psychology and Neurodiversity

By Gemma Sandwell

I didn't know I was neurodivergent until my early thirties, when I found out everything all started to make sense and slot into place. This led me onto a journey of running an aligned business, doing a TEDx and overcoming extreme anxiety. Positive Psychology was one of the tools I used to get me there. But first…

Let me take you back to my school years, this is when the feeling started that I had something wrong with me, I was bullied at school and the kids used to say I had something wrong with me, pick on me for my appearance. There was even an occasion where an adult picked on me at school.

A theatre production came to visit the school one day to promote healthy eating and gave each child at the school an apple, we had to eat the apple and say how we felt eating it…

The lady running the theatre production looked around the room, creeping death, silence, every child I felt was thinking 'dear god, please not me' and she honed in on me, my stomach dropped through the floor and my head started to spin.

'How did the apple taste?' She barked at me…

I felt the blush come into my cheeks and my heart started pounding in my head…

I croaked the word 'nice' out of my mouth.

'Niceeeee?!!' She barked, 'Niceeeee? What kind of a word is niceee?!' I wanted the floor to open up and swallow me, tears formed in my eyes, why did she have to pick on me and why couldn't I do better?! What on earth was wrong with me? The children around me started laughing at me, it was like a horror movie with an evil clown laughing at me and everyone joining in, I still remember this clear as day to this day.

These 'episodes' where I continually felt like I had something wrong with me continued through most of my childhood and into adulthood. I didn't speak up about how I felt, I pushed myself through school, college, university and work where I worked my way up the corporate ladder in HR to try and 'do better'.

I was bullied in the workplace for being 'too sensitive' and 'too nice'. One woman in a project meeting strangely mirroring the woman from the apple fiasco (even had a similar haircut) barked at me 'you're too nice Gemma, being nice is not going to get this project done!'

As I worked my way up the corporate ladder my health took a hit and it was becoming increasingly harder to commute to and work in London and make it through the week. The weekends consisted of either pushing through and drinking alcohol to numb or cancelling plans with family and friends.

Eventually it all got on top of me and I broke, literally floored with anxiety. I was cooking dinner one night and as I was being present with cooking mindfully stir-frying vegetables it all hit me, I couldn't carry on like this, I sobbed and sobbed and I fell to the floor, dinner burning and the smoke alarm blaring.

I knew there had to be a different way and I went to the doctors for help. I was told that I had anxiety and just needed some anxiety medication to help me carry on every day, to block those sensations I was feeling so I could just carry on.

As I sat in the car tears streaming down my face, I felt an inner knowing, I wasn't broken, why on earth would I block my feelings? This doesn't feel right at all.

I made the decision that day to rip up the prescription and 'heal' myself. With the help of a friend who was a hypnotherapist and armed with my journal and awareness of shadow work I was able to tune into what was going on for me really and start to tune into what I needed.

Shadow work (the term coined by Psychologist Carl Jung) is about parts of ourselves we have pushed down, usually we are told as a child these parts of us our not desirable and we shouldn't be a certain way or through traumatic experiences we pushed things into our subconscious mind to keep us safe. Through doing shadow work and looking at perceived negative feelings and emotions and allowing them to be there we bring to light those parts of us and we balance the energy of them. For example, when I considered on some level that I actually desired to have anxiety (subconsciously) because otherwise it wouldn't be there this shifted everything for me.

It wasn't long after I was driving along a country lane and I was listening to a podcast and the presenter mentioned something about being HSP, she spoke about her intense emotions, empathy and picking up energy from people and busy places. I googled this term as I didn't know what it was and I realised it was talking about me!

The Highly Sensitive Person (HSP) term coined by Elaine Aron is someone who is born with simply more processing receptors in the brain. We literally take in more information from the world around us, we pick up energy and emotions from others easily and feel things like music and art on a deeper level due to the depth of processing.

Being HSP also means you are an empath which is a term more widely used. Empathy can be developed more through life experiences through and trauma. All the 'trauma' I'd tried to heal was just neurodiversity. All the anxiety that I thought meant I had something wrong with me was actually just my natural innate sensitivities. I read that 15-20% of all mammals are sensitive as an evolutionary advantage to protect the tribe from danger and I continued to research this trait.

From that day forward I vowed to take better care of myself and on a quest to help others I reached out on social media and I held interviews with other sensitive women about how they felt and what support they needed. This was not only incredibly validating for me and my experience but I found my tribe of people and I started to build up some strategies to support myself and others.

I started to build better boundaries into my life and I managed to negotiate working from home most of the time so I could be away from the sensory overwhelm of the city, office and the commute. When I was working in London, I allowed more time and only booked a certain hotel I felt comfortable in near the river and had extra time in parks and walking (moving my body and energy!).

This also gave me headspace to grow my business where I was running courses, programmes and coaching for fellow HSPs and Intuitive Business owners. I also did a TEDx in front of thousands of people which I thought I'd never have the confidence to do. Having this knowledge and self-care practices around it helped me tap into the gifts of my sensitivities (as my fight/flight response wasn't activated all the time I could actually tune into my intuition, which I felt on a deep level, and take into action the guidance I had). I used a few strategies which helped me with my sensitivities which shifted a lot for me and my business.

Part of these strategies was something I had learned a few years earlier and hadn't even realised was helping with my neurodiversity, that was Positive Psychology. I studied Psychology for my degree and a couple of years later a psychology friend (Sue Langley CEO of the Langley Group who are leading the way for Positive Psychology in Australia) got in touch to say she was running one of the first Positive Psychology courses in the UK. I jumped at the chance to study this as it felt new and exciting and the rebel in me liked that it was challenging the norm when it came to Psychology!

Positive Psychology focuses on human flourishing and looks at all emotions as valid but has found real success through leveraging Positive Emotions. It focuses on what is right with people (whereas traditional psychology focuses on what is wrong and looks to fix it!). When I started to tap into my Strengths and what was 'right' with me this started to shift everything as well as including the incredible Positive Psychology practices in my life such as gratitude and Mindfulness which were very inextricably linked.

I realised that I could just be myself and I had unique strengths no one else had, I was incredibly intuitive, I could know what someone was feeling and what was going on for them without them saying a thing, I'd feel the energy of a room, I'd know in a group of people I was training what was needed and how to shift the energy and I was really good at seeing other people's strengths and zooming out and seeing the bigger picture. I hope as you're reading this, I hope you realise you have unique strengths too!

Positive Psychology helps us when we are sensitive because for most of us the fight/flight centre of the brain is more active due to having more sensory processing receptors in our brain. This is why we are much more likely to get overstimulated when there is lots of sensory input going on at once. For me if I go to someone's house and the radio is on and the TV and the kids are screaming this is all too much noise and I soon reach a point where my brain shuts down, I go all foggy and I can't concentrate.

(Equally those extra sensory processors love some beautiful music, happy crowds at a festival and a good noisy firework display! So, we do seek out sensory input that feels good to us too!)

Positive Psychology helps because the feel-good emotions that come from using this technique in human flourishing and using our strengths releases neurotransmitters in our brains which fuel the parts of the brain responsible for creativity and problem solving and helps shut down the fight/flight centre. This is how we build Positive Resilience and it has been found through Positive Psychology research that the phrase 'What doesn't kill you makes you stronger' isn't necessarily true. Yes, we can have lessons from these times but it's actually building Positive resilience in the brain which makes a difference, focusing on what's right with us, our strengths and our gifts.

Positive Resilience works, especially as a neurodivergent and in my case a HSP because a lot of the time we have more activated fight/flight centres, we are born sensitive into a world not designed for our sensitivities so everything feels at 100% volume and the brain doesn't know the difference between a tiger attacking us and us feeling overwhelmed (neuroscientifically it's the same threat!). So, by using Positive Psychology we can fuel the areas of the brain that help us move forward in a calmer place, much able to deal with what life throws at us.

This is the key to human flourishing, especially as a neurodivergent.

Lastly, I want to mention boundaries, it is important for anyone to have boundaries around what they need as their authentic selves but even more important for neurodivergence. If you are sensitive then it is a journey to setting boundaries around your needs, this might look like leaving a party early if it's too overwhelming, saying no to certain things that overwhelm you (and getting to grips with being okay with that, for many years I thought it was bolder and stronger to push on through because of the mental health narrative out there but this just made it all worse!).

As you can tell from my story, it's been a journey and I'm still evolving and learning as I go. Positive Psychology was that initial spark and bringing it together with the tools such as Shadow Work and the realisation of energy I was picking up and the boundaries I needed was key.

So, what are your strengths? What do you love to do? What are the gifts of your neurodivergence? I invite you to consider how you can tap into Positive Emotion daily too, it will make a big difference.

If you'd like to research more about being HSP you can head to https://hsperson.com/test/

If you'd like some support you can reach out to me here www.gemmasandwell.com or email me gemma@gemmasandwell.com

Watch my TEDx here
https://www.youtube.com/watch?v=D3-8E_zn9bQ

Didi Kan's Bio

Didi Kan is a Clinical Hypnotherapist, Rapid Transformational Therapist (RTT), author, coach and content creator, who specialises in depression, anxiety, stress, addiction and self-sabotage.

After spending a vast majority of his life suffering from Bipolar Disorder, Borderline Personality Disorder, Attention Deficit Hyperactive Disorder, Complex Traumatic Stress Disorder, addiction to class A drugs, alcohol, cigarettes, anger, sex, overthinking and the most crippling and corrosive insecurities and reactivity, Didi experienced his own transformation. Ever since he has been on a mission to share his experience, expertise and passion to help people heal from the past, find happiness, peace and purpose, and enhance all aspects of their life from the place where everything starts and ends: the mind.

Neurodiversity And Us is his 8th collaboration with the And Us book series, and a continuation of his conversation with Us.

If you have enjoyed his contribution to Neurodiversity And Us, please feel welcome to find out more about him as a transformational therapist and coach, and follow his journey as an author and content creator on social media. All details and links are to be found and regularly updated on his website:

□ didikantransformation.com
www.didikantransformation.com

YouTube □ Didi Kan @didikan1147
Facebook □
https://www.facebook.com/didikantransformation
Tiktok □ @DidiKanTransformation
Instagram □ @DidiKanTransformation
LinkedIn □ Didi Kan

PS: In the picture from left: Matt, Doggos Lily and Alfie, Didi.

Chapter Three

We Are All The Continuation Of A Story

By Didi Kan

Every single one of us is the random result of the big lottery of the universe. As we begin our human adventure, we all start somewhere, sometime and in some environment and circumstances we have no control over. We are like stardusts fallen from the sky, at the mercy of the whims of the wind and all the other elements, and a mysterious plan we either call Destiny, Karma, Luck or God. We are all the continuation of a story that started many generations before us. And because that story is unfolding vastly at an unconscious level, we are essentially fulfilling throughout a lifetime a prophecy given to us at birth by our parents, environment and culture, with no conscious awareness of any of it. We are a momentum, an impetus, a chapter from a story so much bigger than us. We are what happened to us and how we deal with life as a result of what happened to us. What happened to us happened to us because it happened to our parents, and their parents before them in some way, shape or form. And the way we deal with life is an unfolding of what was learnt and observed of our caregivers dealing with their own life.

Trauma Is Transformative And Generational

Many people try to understand the origins of why people are different neurologically, and try to classify them within the nature versus nurture dichotomy. I personally believe that this shouldn't matter so much. Nature and nurture only indicate whether traumas and limiting beliefs have occurred in the timeline of our story before or after we are born. Either way, the traumas and limiting beliefs that determine the course of our life end up affecting us in the very same way eventually. One of the ways to look at traumas is to see them as the response to an overwhelm of unregulated stress, that changes the structure of our brain. And so, traumas can not only be born from abuse or neglect during our developmental years, but they can also be inherited, as in passed on genetically through our DNA, or acquired culturally through the perpetuating of traditional limiting beliefs, and the normalisation of long-established toxic behaviours, like a generational curse flowing through the bloodline of our tribe. In other words, all mental disorders are an adaptation and evolution of some sort of trauma that occurred sometime during our childhood, during our time spent in our mother's womb, or throughout our ancestors' lives. Some may argue that traumas also occur in adulthood, and they do. But the reason why some people suffer from PTSD while some others exposed to the same event don't, is because of an absence of coping mechanism. In other words, those with a background of trauma, such as an unstable upbringing, are more vulnerable to overwhelming stress in adulthood, and prone to Post Traumatic Stress Disorder or PTSD. Which brings us back to the notion that trauma lives on a timeline, and can even travel through generations if not addressed.

Neurodiversity

There are many types of mental disorders and many systems of classifications for them. Bipolar disorder for instance is a mood disorder, that is typically characterised by random fluctuations between manic and grandiose episodes, and periods of intense depression with suicidal ideation. Borderline Personality Disorder is a personality disorder characterised by fear of abandonment, emotional instability and disturbed patterns of thinking. ADHD is a neurodevelopmental disorder that affects focus, organisational, time management and stress coping skills amongst many things. Complex PTSD (CPTSD) is an anxiety disorder that affects our sense of worthiness, our ability to trust others and feel safe, and our relationship with the world and people. All those conditions vary in symptoms from an individual to another, have many overlaps, and can often be comorbidities. In other words, it is not uncommon to have more than one condition. And because the brain is plastic in nature, therefore designed to constantly change and adapt to our thoughts, observations and experiences, all conditions can be classified as neurodivergent, since people who have those conditions do not experience life, people, reality and relationships like people who haven't got those conditions do. Their brain as a result has evolved to function differently. And the reason I have chosen those 4 examples specifically is because I have suffered from them all, which puts me in an advantageous position to talk about them from a human and emotional perspective.

The Gift Of Awareness

I have been diagnosed and treated for suicidal manic depression as a teenager, which is what bipolar disorder was called originally, so I always knew that I was officially different to "normal" people. I was extremely insecure, emotionally fragile, unstable and reactive, obsessed with overthinking, unfairness and revenge, and terribly pessimistic, depressed and sad. It took me many more years however to realise that I also suffered from borderline personality disorder, ADHD and CPTSD. I haven't had a chance to do the full tests yet at the time I am writing this, and I will most probably go down that route when the opportunity arises. But I don't need the opinion of anyone else to KNOW already that I suffered all those conditions. Because now in my 50s, I have spent my entire adult life studying, analysing and trying to understand myself, the world of people, and the abysmal mysterious discrepancy between me and it. I have suffered tremendously from my exposure to people, I have always felt like an alien in regards to the codes of conduct, behaviour and interaction in society everyone seems to understand instinctively and follow naturally, including within my own family. Being told often as a joke by my Mum that they picked up the wrong baby at the hospital, a part of me actually did believe this. I never fitted into this world, I always felt like an outcast, a stranger, an impostor. The other reason "I know" is because I have worked with enough people suffering from those conditions to recognise the symptoms within me. Us therapists are sometimes so consumed with helping others that we forget to look in the mirror, and realise that we could be suffering from the same problems. I can still remember the day I had my epiphany during the Covid pandemic. We have found out that my husband Matt was on the autistic spectrum and that I had BPD and ADHD, on top of my Bipolar, thanks to TikTok. With a little self-reflection, inner investigations and meditation work, I realised that I have suffered from CPTSD for many years too, and I also remembered that I had Tourettes and Obsessive-Compulsive Disorder or OCD during a period of my life. From that point onwards everything made sense. It is as if I went through an exhilarating tunnel of crystal-clear flashbacks, with the revelation as to why every single one of those events happened, like in some movies with a major twist, unveiling the crucial missing piece of the puzzle at the very end, and leaving the audience in shock, elation and lucidity.

A New Source Of Information

TikTok has been a game changer as the world has never seen such plethora of information, delivered directly from the vast trenches of the neurodiverse community. Of course, as with all platforms, there are all sorts of individuals, preaching all sorts of things, with various levels of veracity and honesty, for all sorts of various motives. But the vast majority of content creators who posts about neurodiversity on TikTok do bring something fresh, useful, valuable and even life changing for some. They bring us vulnerability, experience and aha moments. They teach us either compassion and kindness, or self-reflection if we can relate to them. They tell us about life stories no book has ever written about. Because it is paramount to highlight that the understanding of mental health and the design and implementation of effective strategies to improve mental health are a relatively recent occurrence. Information about mental health is scarce, anecdotal and clinical, and there is still a lot of work to be done, not only at a professional and academic level, but also from a societal perspective. What we know about the mind has only been accurate and useful in the last few decades, thanks to the advances in technology, allowing us to actually see what happens in the brain, instead of making wild assumptions, influenced by biased moral values and old prejudices.

The Dismantling Of Past Toxicities

Until 1987 for instance homosexuality was still considered a mental illness, to be treated with electro shocks or punished with chemical castration. I was seventeen years old then, and up till this point I grew up watching television shows demonising Gays as either mentally ill, or evil perverted pedophiles, on a mission to assault all children and spread AIDS. This was not so long ago, yet this mere example demonstrates how medieval, barbaric and ignorant mental health professionals and academics have been all that time. Sadly, many things that are still being taught in psychology curriculum and being promoted in the media today are perpetuating outdated, erroneous and even dangerous beliefs. Take those who are still preaching toxic masculinity, patriarchy and the conservation of traditional values for instance, they are using the same fear propagandas, scapegoatism tactics, and fake virtue and heroism gratification system to divide, control and manipulate the masses, that men have been using for millennia with Religion. And sadly, too many people are still falling for them. Unbeknown to the fact that they are only attracted to those ideologies because their subconscious mind recognises those familiar feelings of fear, hatred, disgust and anger they grew up with. This has got nothing to do with logic, reason, truth or right versus wrong. We are creatures of emotions and feelings first and foremost. We are not thinking beings that feel. We are feeling beings that think, and we find appealing whatever feels familiar. And so if bullying, blaming and scapegoatism were a familiar occurrence during our childhood for instance, our subconscious mind will look out for any reasons and pretexts to bully, blame and scapegoat, in order to emulate those same familiar emotions from the past. Next, the brain, our rational mind, will come up with a narrative, excuses and justifications to back up those choices. And that explains how Trans people have become the new Gays. Any excuses to demonise and persecute Trans people, no matter how lame or irrational the excuses may be, are celebrated by the reactive and blood thirsty masses, in need of triggers for their addiction to fear, hatred, disgust and anger. History is repeating itself. Albeit one important detail though: the existence, power, speed and transparency of social media and the internet. Technology is enabling us to expose and correct obsolete normalities such as racism, sexism, homophobia, transphobia, ableism, fat shaming, etc... The world is changing for the better and it is a pleasure to witness. But the way it has behaved in the last 2000 years explains categorically the proliferation and normalisation of suffering, traumas, and the resulting plague of mental and emotional distress and disorders.

Awareness Is Not Self Diagnosis

Now of course, going back to general mental health, we don't want to self diagnose. We want to ask new questions, and open our mind to exploring different aspects and possibilities about ourselves. Although there will always be a minority of people misusing the internet, I do strongly believe however that the vast majority of those who discovered they were neurodivergent, or suffering from mental disorders via TikTok, regardless of their age, KNEW, and had similar epiphanies than we had when we found out about ourselves my husband and I. When we know we just know. It hits you like a lightning bolt that switches on a light bulb in your head, and suddenly we can see clearly and everything finally makes sense. And unless you are a neurodivergent person who recently realised they were neurodivergent all along, it would be challenging to explain this to a neurotypical person. Realising that we are neurodivergent after a lifetime of believing that we were stupid, lazy, needy or weak provides us with an explanation, a passport, an ID, a justification and authorisation to exist in this world, without feeling inferior, lesser or lower class citizens. It brings solace, relief and liberation from a lifetime of guilt, shame, self hatred, depression and not enough ness. It is freedom from believing that there was something wrong about us, and the immense realisation that all of our suffering was the result of an ignorant world that didn't know how to love us.

A Tradition Of Judgement

We are influenced from a young age to believe that there are some things we should be, do and have, whilst some other things are off limit to us. Most of all we are conditioned to have expectations, based on what is perceived as normal. In other words, everyone in society is programmed to expect everyone to behave like everyone else, or else there is something wrong with them. And because most societies all over the world in the last 2000 years have been built and shaped by organised corrupted religions, structured on a blame, guilt and shame system, under that light it is easy to see why there has been so little progress in the fields of mental health. Why try to understand when we can judge ? Under a system that came up with a fixed set of virtues and sins, men needed sinners to award the righteous, validate their principles, and strengthen their control.

We Are All Enough
Until Society Tells Us Otherwise

All my life I have been judged, condemned and blamed for things that I could do nothing about. Just like all neurodivergent people and anyone who suffers from any type of mental disorder, our suffering comes from the judgement of others, not from the condition itself. Because although the disorder may be mental, we can not suffer mentally. Suffering is emotional. Suffering happens in the body through the language of feelings and sensations. Mental limitations only prevents us to do or perceive certain things. The frustration is emotional and comes from comparison. Unmet expectations born from a lack of support, understanding and compassion, and borrowed expectations from others that were never for us to fulfil. Someone with learning disabilities for instance may struggle communicating with others and completing mundane tasks, but until they feel that they are being judged for not meeting the neurotypical standards and expectations, they actually don't suffer from their learning disability. The notion of not enough ness comes from the neurotypical paradigm. If we can provide strategies, guidance and assistance so that neurodivergent people can live their most fulfilling life, void of unmet expectations, guilt, shame or pressure, their neurodivergence is not a problem. It is just a different way to live a life. Merely an alternative lifestyle. And it is down to society to make this happen.

There Are No Sinners, Only Scapegoats

I have been judged and called unpredictable, unhinged, unreliable and insane because of the manic episodes caused by the bipolar disorder. I have been called a liar and a fantasist because of the grandiosity that comes with it. I came across as miserable, joy killer and negative when I went into periods of devastating depression. Because of the CPTSD I have also been judged and called shy, antisocial, weird and paranoid. Because of the ADHD I have been judged and called lazy, stupid, disrespectful for always being late and good for nothing. Because of the Borderline I have been judged and called insecure, desperate, needy, nasty, petty, vindictive and downright bad. Finally, because of the addictions to drug, alcohol and sex, being the only systems, I knew to stress regulate and self-medicate, and help alleviate the overwhelm caused by all of those things, I was judged and called weak, a loser and a greedy and disgusting pervert. All my entire life I have believed that I was the lowest of the lowest in all the categories of human virtues. And only those who have experienced the same can comprehend how tortuous and soul destroying this is. I never chose any of my mental disorders, nor the adaptational coping mechanisms. Yet, like all of my undiagnosed neurodivergent siblings, I have been punished by society every day relentlessly for them.

Choices Exist
But They Are Not Accessible To All

And the reason for this is because we are being taught that people always have a choice, do everything on purpose, and that their choices reflect their character, true nature and intentions. We can choose to be brave or scared, angry or respectful, positive or miserable, intelligent or stupid, sensible or irresponsible, calm or hysterical, strong or weak… and whichever choice we make is really only about right or wrong… our choices are labels and measures of our quality, value and potential as a human being, because we believe in some universal free will, some mythological birth given willpower everyone has access to abundantly. We are conditioned to make immediate assumptions, judge and condemn as our default mode, and we lose our greatest power, our divine capacity for empathy, understanding, connection and healing. Here is a truth not everyone can accept: Not everyone has access to that choice. Not everyone's brain operates in the same way. Not everyone's subconscious mind owns the same baggage, or has adapted to the same traumas and adversities. Every single person's belief system manifests a different reality. And as long as we are unable to look at one another past our own projections, and through the illusions of their perceived behaviours, neurodivergent people will not only believe that they are born inferior, substandard and inadequate, but they will also never get a chance to learn and improve their existence in this society. We must evolve away from the old paradigm of right versus wrong. We must upgrade our standards of "normality".

The Tyranny Of Normality

All concepts exist in contrast to their antagonists. What this means is that there would not be neurodivergent classifications if there weren't neurotypical standards. There can't be mental disorders if there isn't some sort of mental order in the first place. Normality therefore is the original culprit. Do we want anarchy and pandemonium? Of course not. So how do we solve this? By expanding our perception of normality. By expanding our pursuit of acceptance, understanding and compassion. The more we expand through understanding the pool of "us", the smaller there are of "them" left, until we eventually eradicate the notion of "them" altogether. Because if we can look at the world passed the barriers of divisive beliefs, we are all the same. Now, here is a thought: If we know that someone has some sort of learning disability, it is easier for us to be kind, patient and compassionate when they are struggling to do something we are expecting them to do. If we believe that a person is neurotypical however we may not be so lenient, as we may judge them for being stupid, lazy or weak. Where do we draw the line though? Who are we to judge those we can offer compassion to or not? We don't know anyone's background, what happened to them, whether or not they are trapped in some terribly unfortunate circumstances, or if they have been contemplating ending their lives for years? Anyone in this world, including neurotypical people, have their shares of baggage, heartbreaks, limitations and invisible wounds and scars. We all experience anxiety, depression, burnout, loss, confusion, emotional instability or disturbed patterns of thoughts and behaviours, in some capacity and through phases, all throughout our life. And no one could ever tell behind our brave faces. Because we are all conditioned to appear normal for survival. We all mask.

The Case For Anger, Rage And Aggression

Sometimes we can't mask any longer. And for some of us, our traumas can take over and hijack our mind and the direction of our life in spectacular and devastating fashion. Years of frustration and emotional repression can be unleashed in a moment, and manifest themselves through the energy of anger, rage, hatred or even aggression. Those manifestations are the least tolerated in society, because they represent danger, and so they have been traditionally dealt with force, control and submission. Instead of courage, open mind and compassion. How many times have I heard people telling me:" Calm down, don't you dare talk to me like that, lower your tone, I will not tolerate that language…" Unaware of the fact that in those moments, once my emotional mind has taken over, I have absolutely zero control over my behaviour, the things I say and the way I say them. And the more I am told to calm down, the more I get aggravated. Because in those moments, to me "calm down" means "your feelings don't matter to me, YOU don't matter to me. Be quiet. I don't care about your pain or what you have to say because you are an inferior human being".

We Can Only Give
What We Have Been Given

I remember having manic episodes and doing and saying irrational and hurtful things to others. I remember taking the most insignificant comments personally all the time by strangers, and being obsessed with revenge. I remember leaving thousands of messages on the answerphone machine, or sending thousands of texts messages for days on end, and blackmailing those I loved and loved me in the cruellest and pettiest ways. I remember losing control every night and causing fights, havoc and troubles wherever I went, forgetting all about it the next day, and starting all over again the following evening… and the only reason I ever did what I did, time and again, is because I didn't know any better. There have been moments of mental clarity when I realised what I was doing, and I hated myself for that. I hated my life. I hated people. I hated the whole world. And most of all I hated my inability to change. Because just like anybody else I need to be seen and heard. I need to belong somehow. I need to know that I exist through the eyes of others. And the only way I knew how to do that back then was through the energy of rage, desperation and drama. If I knew how to engage with people through the energy of love and kindness, I would have chosen that option without hesitation. But I didn't have love or kindness. Because I have not been given love or kindness.

Compassion, understanding, forgiveness and oneness are the future of humankind.

I have now learnt and even become proficient at loving and being kind. I even made it a career, teaching people who need love and kindness how to find it within themselves. But it is paramount to understand that we can only give what we own, and we only own what we have been given. Criminals only become criminals because they believe that this is who they are, and that anything else is not available to them. Having said that it is important to highlight that we can all learn in some capacity, given the right circumstances. We can all change in some capacity. We can all adapt and grow in some capacity. But for this to happen EVERYONE must be treated like equal human beings who need and deserve unconditional help, support, love and guidance, REGARDLESS of their neurological profile. Not like people who choose to do "bad things" because they are inherently evil or weak, unless they have a disabled pass. There is not a single person in prison for instance that hasn't suffered from the generational trauma I talked about earlier in my chapter in this book, and been subsequently victim of a system, that thrives on finding, demonising, dehumanising and punishing scapegoats, by turning them into the bad people they need to complete their narrative. Because no one has ever chosen consciously and deliberately to be in prison. If a crime has been committed of course we must all abide by the laws of men. But any criminal should be given access to some level of rehabilitation. Just like all families of victims should also be given a chance to try and understand, forgive and resume a better life. And what's more we can prevent the next generations to fall into the same trap.

Conclusion

Nothing was ever our fault. Because not everything has to be the fault of something or someone. The universe is chaos. There is no fault. Only cause and effect. Only a picture bigger than the puny confines of our human fears and judgments. Only chains of events for us to decipher, understand, learn, grow and evolve from. In other words, when society is finally ready to evolve away from a toxic tradition of judgement, guilt and shame, and replace it with a system that includes, welcomes, respects and supports the specific requirements of ALL people, including neurodivergent people, there will simply no longer be any mental or emotional disorders. There will only be people, who are either neurotypical or neurodivergent, thriving together in a society big enough, generous enough and kind enough for all.

Interlude Two

By Roy Payamal

"Everybody sings a song. Played on a guitar that never was. The strings untuned so you can only play it without the chords. It doesn't matter anyway as there wasn't a song sung or written in the first place coz I heard the singer lost her voice… I took a book for a walk and I lost my way. The pages crumpled before I reached the end. But a friend who did told me it was a blank."

Facebook: www.facebook.com/roy.payamal

Interlude Three

Each One of You Unique

By Mamie Philp

You answered questions eloquently during class discussions
But failed the test because the words were a jumble;
So, we did it again with a reader and scribe
And you passed with flying colours.
You said the colour blue sent your anxiety levels sky high
And you couldn't see the text and pictures;
So, I changed the background colour on all my slides
Transforming your experience.

You knocked all the colouring pens off the table
And apologised profusely;
Then we picked them up together
Because you had done nothing wrong.
You didn't like being singled out to speak in
class
Even though you knew the answers;
So, we'd chat things through one-to-one
Or wait for the results of your creativity.
Others too close made you nervous,
You needed your own space;
So, you chose your desk and we moved it
To a position that felt safe.
Surrounded by so many people
The classroom got too noisy;
So, to let you concentrate in silence
I let you wear your headphones.
You often found it hard to focus,
Your mind jumping from one thing to the next;
So, I broke down tasks into smaller chunks
And let you doodle when you wanted.
You wouldn't look me in the eye or smile
When I explained things;
There was no need to take offence
Because I knew that was your style.
Sometimes you were a fidget,
A distraction for the class;
So, I let you go for a walk
To help you release some energy.
You would forget to do things
And the pile of undid tasks got bigger;
So, we put together a diary
That would help you to remember.
You liked to have routine

And to do things your own way;
So, I set out lesson structures with
Boundaries for you agreed.
    Your attention to detail meant nothing would be
missed,
    Incisive questions and commentary,
    Challenging points of view,
    Giving richness to debate.
    A group of individuals making up a class;
    Neurodiverse and not, each one of you unique.
    A teacher not always getting it right,
    Doing their best to meet your needs.

Tal's Bio

"We're just navigating life, whatever our brain wiring" - coined by Tal.

Tal was born in the UK to an American father and an Israeli mother. By her late teens she knew that I wanted to investigate fraud on the stock and currency markets. She qualified as a lawyer in order to do that job and by her early 20s, she was!

Tal met her husband in 2001 and their first son was born in 2007, with the second arriving in 2009. Shortly after their first son's birth both her husband and she were made redundant and shortly after their second son's birth her mother died. Those were pretty emotionally (and financially) difficult years.

Since writing her chapter, Tal has left the Police in order to work for a local government council, in a role where the primary aim is to get young, neurodiverse, people into work. That's how much she loved setting up the Police Neurodiverse Internship Scheme.

Their son's diagnosis has had an impact on so much of our lives, individually and as a family. Both she and her husband now work with a large number of Neurodiverse people. Their older son's friendship group contains a number of young people who are comfortable in their neurodiversity.

Tal has a view of parenting and relating to one's child that lifts and dispels any negativity surrounding the role of a parent of a child on the spectrum. She is a childhood friend who tells me that her mother lived by the mantra, "everything happens for a reason." Given the choices Tal has made about the direction she wanted her professional life to take since her son received his diagnosis, she now firmly believes she knows the answer to the question she asked herself at the time, "why me?" Because she is determined to be one of the individuals who encourages employers to reconsider *their* perceptions of how much neurodiverse people can achieve. Her son, Becky and the young people she is helping find paid work in her current job, are the people who prove her point. In her own (and her mother's) words, she's found the reason she's on this planet!

Tal volunteers at https://spaceherts.org.uk/
Find Tal on LinkedIn

https://www.linkedin.com/in/tal-stein-7a56b53a

Chapter Four

Positives Out Of Negatives

By Tal Stein

The Negative Power (Of Secrets)

Like many, I grew up in a somewhat dysfunctional family. What I didn't realise until my mid-teens is that dysfunction had also included an awful lot of secrets. When I was 15 my mother had taken me to visit my paternal grandparents and uncles during a trip to America, and left me with them for a few days, so that I could get to know them better. It was during that time that they told me 'truths' that didn't match what I'd been told by my parents as I was growing up.

Coming home from that trip I did a lot of thinking and processing. When I confronted my mother, she did then give me 'truths' that matched what my American family had told me. When I confronted my father, initially he got verbally angry, and then just went silent and wouldn't engage in the conversation at all.

What I learnt from that summer was the destructive power that secrets can hold. I vowed that I was never going to live like that, ever!

Diagnosis

Fast forward several decades and my husband and I by then have a six-year-old son who is developing and behaving entirely 'normally' and a 4-year-old who is definitely not! I am a qualified lawyer who only ever wanted to work as a fraud investigator, and that is what I did. So, with that investigative background, I started trying to work out why our younger son behaved so oddly so much of the time. Two years of reading, going on courses, approaching NHS doctors and eventually, going private and paying, we got a diagnosis - Autism and Attention Deficit Hyperactivity Disorder (ADHD). Finally, we had answers!

The Psychiatrist who diagnosed our son was fantastic, and I still have the doodles he drew for us as he explained about the lack of executive function that was one of the biggest problem areas for our son. He did give us a very thorough, albeit very negative ("Your son's school years will be a nightmare for you and for him") description, of what lay ahead of us. And that was it. No more. No support, no suggestions of where we could look for further guidance or education (for us on how to parent him.) Just a great deal of pressure to immediately put our son on ADHD drugs.

I felt utterly swamped. I remember describing it to a friend by saying, it's as if we'd walked out of the Psychiatrist's office, at the bottom of a very, very steep mountain. At the top of that mountain was snow, lots of it, and at any given moment it felt as if the snow would come whooshing down that mountain and swamp us! It was either that or somehow find a way to climb to the top of that mountain and conquer it. Either option was utterly terrifying and very isolating.

When we got our son's diagnosis, and knowing my feelings about secrets, my husband and I didn't even consider NOT telling our son his diagnosis. However, we waited a week in order to get appropriate books for both our Neurotypical older boy and our Neurodiverse younger son. (Medikidz is an incredibly brilliant range of comic-type books covering a huge number of illnesses and conditions. We got the relevant ones for our younger boy.) We also took the boys to see Pixar's Inside Out - a movie about the emotions operating inside a little girl's head, for the younger one's 6th birthday treat.

As soon as we got home from the movie, we sat the boys down and I explained that actually, there should have been a sixth character inside the little girl's head, and it should have been called 'Executive Function' and that in my son's head, that character was much, much smaller than all the other emotions. And that's one reason why he found so many aspects of growing up so difficult. And the name for that was called Autism. He sat there, very still (with ADHD he never, ever does that!) Then he looked at me, with total joy on his face and said, repeatedly, "Mummy, it's not my fault. MUMMY, IT'S NOT MY FAULT!!" The relief on his face and in his body as he said that made me know, absolutely and totally, that telling him was the right thing to have done. Whilst I can understand others not wanting to tell their child, with my experience of secrets and their destructive power, there was no way I wasn't going to tell my child. I wanted him to control his autism, not allow his autism to control him! The next thing I did was send an email to my entire extended family explaining his diagnosis and making it very clear that if they invited us to a family gathering, then they did so, accepting my son's behaviour. If they didn't want the behaviour, then don't invite us. 95% of mine and my husband's families were totally accepting and welcoming and have continued to be. For the other 5%, contact was pretty minimal before and that simply carried on!

As for the ADHD drugs, I refused to consider them for a long time. I wanted to see what knowledge by us, by his (mainstream, primary) school, his grandparents and his out-of-school activities could achieve now that we knew why he behaved the way he did. Those changes in parenting and schooling strategies did improve some elements of his behaviour, but not all. Eventually, the school asked me to at least try ADHD medications with my son to see what difference they might make. I was terrified that I'd end up with a zombie, as that was all I'd, at that time, heard about Ritalin.

My son was initially put on a very small dose of a Ritalin-derived drug. We gave him the first dose on a Monday morning at 7:30 am. An hour later I'm walking him to school and he suddenly looks at me and says, "Mummy, can I tell you about Wolverine? He's got special powers and he can do......." I'd zoned out by that stage! All I was thinking was,

'OMG, my son is talking in a coherent sentence for the first time in his life! I can follow what he's saying! And if I'm not lost and confused, desperately trying to follow the 10,000 threads of thoughts that are constantly whizzing around his head, then he probably isn't either! OMG!!" As any 'guilt-seeking' mother tends to do, I then felt guilty for not putting him on the ADHD drugs earlier, but with calm hindsight, I do know we did the right thing in waiting and learning and getting acclimatised to what an Autism and ADHD diagnosis actually meant for our son and our family.

"Selling" The Positive

At some point in this acclimatisation process, I came across the Autism Research Centre, which was constantly looking for volunteers to participate in research projects that were being run through it. My husband is a scientist, so when I asked my younger son if he would be willing to help other scientists learn more about Autism, he was quite keen anyway. When I explained that as his was the only autistic brain in the family, he was therefore the only one who could help those other scientists, he became even more willing to help. This wasn't an accidental step. I did it very intentionally. I wanted our son to view his autism in a positive light, not in a debilitating or negative way.

The daughter of friends of ours has Cerebral Palsy and whilst she could use crutches when she was younger, she will, as she grows older, be more and more dependent on a wheelchair. Her family do not treat her as disabled. She does not consider her disability to be a negative thing: She has competed for Great Britain in the Paralympics and as a teenager she told me that she wanted to be a surgeon. I asked her how she would conduct surgery from a wheelchair. "I'll get a hydraulic one, then I can be at whatever height I need to be to do the surgery!" That was the positive, problem-solving, mindset I wanted to instil in our son, right from the

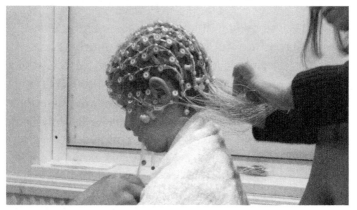

very start.

The very first piece of research my son took part in involved measuring his brain activity whilst he undertook a number of different tasks. The picture above shows the researchers getting him prepared. He absolutely loved it! And that meant that going forward, especially as he's now a teenager, he remembers the positives he associated with his diagnoses from those very early days after we learnt about, what we called then, his 'weirdly wired brain'. Nowadays, I show him the emails that come in that are relevant to his type of diagnosis and his age and he says whether or not he wants to be involved in that research. Recently researchers asked for the parents/carers of autistic children and young people to be participants. I agreed and undertook a morning of quite similar tests to the ones I remember my son doing when he was rigged up in the photo above. (I didn't get the same process, but my eye movements were recorded and the time it took me to complete various tasks.) Again, I volunteered, and talked about it at home that night, so that my son could see that I 'walked his walk' and not just 'talked the talk'. If he can help scientists and researchers, and then when they want parents and carer volunteers, so can I.

Because I'm not reticent or secretive (or negative) about my son's diagnosis, I've been asked to give Neurodiversity training sessions at work: to new police officers, to the call handlers who are the people who answer the '999' calls and to experienced police officers. That last group are actually the hardest to give training sessions for. They think they know everything and have handled every possible situation so they often 'blank out' most of the training session. Interestingly, I've had a few probationers, who get teamed up in their early days with those experienced officers, who remember something I've covered in one of my training sessions when they encounter a person being 'difficult'. Once they've made some of the adaptations I suggested in my training, suddenly they find that the person being 'difficult' isn't being difficult at all. They are very stressed, by a, for them, utterly overwhelming situation and they have none of the coping, or communication, skills that a neurotypical person might have. The probationer then deals with the situation very well and the experienced officer is left writing up a positive report on the newby, and sometimes, somewhat sheepishly, then contacts me for a reminder of what they dismissed out of hand when they were in my training the first time!

To be fair to my policing colleagues, many, many of them are very willing to accept diversity and adapt their behaviour (once they know what adaptations a situation may require), happily and swiftly. There is also a high level of acceptance at all ranks, at least that is what I encountered when I made a suggestion in January 2021.

Acceptance Is Key

I had a new manager and we were having a 'getting to know you' conversation. He bemoaned the fact that he'd lost half his northern team (I was in his southern team) as they had left the Police after 12-18 months of working on very, very repetitive tasks that didn't need to be undertaken by experienced investigators but there was no one else available of a lower rank/experience who could do it.

As a result of all the research, reading and courses I'd attended, I had set up a number of events where Neurodiverse and Neurotypical young people could mix and do activities together. I had arranged them through the small, local autism charity that had helped our family as we started to acclimatise to our son's diagnosis, and my older boy's Scout group. One of the events consisted of the two groups doing all sorts of outdoor activities in a Scout camp - climbing trees, making fires, cooking marshmallows over the fire and building shelters. Ok, these were all 'normal' activities for the Scouts, but totally new and exciting for the Neurodiverse youngsters. I had provided some training to the Scouts in advance, explaining at a very basic level, about how a Neurodiverse brain functions differently and what changes they would need to make in how they spoke and how they behaved, to make the day a bit easier for the Neurodiverse young people, and let them enjoy it as fully as possible.

At the end of the day - which all the kids had really enjoyed - there was a Dad with a large car, clearly taking a number of the Scouts back to their homes. One of the Scouts in the car asked him to stop when he was level with me, and the girl said to me, "they're really not that different from us, are they? I had a really good time today and I hope they all did too."

YES! That is what I want to achieve. That level of acceptance, and recognition, that with a very small amount of adjustments, by the Neurotypical population, who find change much, much easier to do and cope with, everyone can function in their own way and be a productive part of society!

Which leads me back to where I started. When my manager told me about the number of experienced investigators who had left after doing very mundane tasks for long periods of time, knowing, from my research etc, that some Neurodiverse - autistic - people enjoy repetitive tasks, because that gives them the certainty and structure that their brain wiring needs, I suggested that the Police force recruit a couple of people on the autistic spectrum specifically to do those repetitive tasks! My manager looked at me like I'd landed from another planet, but said, "write me up a paper that I can show to more senior officers." So I did.

Shortly after this, a very high-ranking officer made a reference in a Conference where he was giving a speech, of the need for the Police generally, to "embrace whacky thinking." He went on to recognise that the Police "lose the possibility of employing all sorts of brilliant people if we insist on only employing those who think in a particular way." I took one look at my manager and suggested I send the paper I'd written directly to that very high-ranking officer. My manager said, "yes, do it today whilst his words are fresh in his mind." I did. That senior officer has supported me every step of the way, as did many other senior officers.

Supported Internship Scheme
Within The Police

Within three months of me making that suggestion, my original idea had become a Supported Internship Scheme. The Police paired up with a specialist educational college which runs a course to get Neurodiverse young people into work. The college provides a Job Coach, who comes with the young person for a 6 - 9 month work placement. Someone from the Police/employer who has a task for the intern, explains to the Job Coach what the task involves, the Job Coach then teaches the intern the task, in very small, incremental steps. The Job Coach initially supervises the intern until it's clear they understand the task inside out, and then steps away so that the intern can gain the confidence that comes from repeatedly doing the task, and doing it correctly. In return, the experienced investigator, or Police Officer, no longer has to spend months doing low-level administrative, repetitive tasks and can get on with being a fully functioning Police officer, because the Neurodiverse Intern is doing those tasks instead. In my case, the intern that I first recruited, regularly completed one of her tasks at a 99.4% accuracy rate. The Police Officer for whom she was doing that work, every month, with that consistent degree of accuracy was thrilled. He made no secret of the fact that she did the work more accurately, and faster, than he did!

I have to say, that at no point when I was making the suggestion and getting the Scheme set up, did anyone, of any rank put any barriers in the way. I met with overwhelming positivity. The general reaction was, "What a brilliant idea. How do we make it happen?" The Scheme was deemed to be so successful that it is continuing into a second year and into more and more Police forces in England. So far, I've had four other forces contact me to learn how they could go about setting up similar schemes in their forces.

The thing that setting the Scheme up really showed me was that for the vast number of people in a work environment, they will accept any good idea that meets a business need. And the vast majority are more than willing to make adjustments to their behaviour, to the way they speak and to their expectations, so long as they've had some explanation as to why they need to adapt, and some training as to how to adapt. I could have been met with a wave of "why do we want 'that sort' in the office? They'll only make more work for me!" But I didn't, not once. All I got was enthusiasm, willingness and acceptance.

From the way the Scheme worked, and how successful it was, anyone who had had any (unspoken to me, at any rate) doubts, could see the benefits to both the Police and to the intern.

What I said in the many, many presentations I gave, to all sorts of Police audiences, when I was trying to get the Scheme up and running, was that I wanted to break the narrative that automatically focuses on what a Neurodiverse person can't do. Instead, I wanted the focus to be on what they could do, often far more accurately and far faster, than a Neurotypical. I often say to my son, "Don't tell me what you can't do. Show me what you can do".

I firmly believe that any reasonable sized business, in pretty much any field, will have low-level, repetitive tasks that the experienced workforce don't want to do, because, for a Neurotypical brain those tasks are BORING! So, recruit some Neurodiverse people who do want to do that kind of task. Not all will, but the same applies to a Neurodiverse person as to a Neurotypical: Find a job that you enjoy, that plays to your strengths, that you do well and accurately. Suddenly coming to work is not a chore but is an enjoyable way to spend a large part of your day/working life. To those individuals who were 'naysayers': suddenly they find that they don't have to do the boring tasks that they always hated having to do at work, because someone else, who does enjoy those tasks, is doing them.

Yes, the Neurodiverse person at work may not join the tea club, they may not join in the social side of work, and they may find 'small talk' very hard to do. But, if they are doing their job well and there is a recognition from the Neurotypicals in the working environment that some people do have differently wired brains and therefore some of the peripheral parts of being at work may be very, very uncomfortable for certain people, does it actually matter?

What matters is acceptance. By all parties. I know for my intern, when she realised that I did accept her precisely as she was, her confidence grew in leaps and bounds. At one point she made a comment to me, that someone listening in would probably have thought, "How can she be so rude to her boss?!" Instead, I just thought, "Oh good, she's relaxed and now knows she can say whatever she wants and I'm not going to be offended. She's found her confidence." And she had. She's now attending job interviews on her own and even had the confidence to call out an interviewer when they behaved totally inappropriately in her interview. She called the company and complained about the interviewer's attitude to her. As far as I'm concerned, I view that as a success. My young, ex-intern, now has a sense of her own self-worth and isn't afraid to protect it.

So, what of the massive, overwhelming, snow-tipped mountain that I first imagined when we got my son's diagnosis seven years ago now? I haven't thought about it for a long time. I no longer feel overwhelmed. I realise that we are in our 'normal', and that's a normal that will change and adapt as our son grows. As any child grows.

One of the courses I attended when we were on our acclimatisation process, spoke of the "Journey of Adjustment," and in that session they gave us the following item. I've never forgotten it because it is so apt.

WELCOME TO HOLLAND by
Emily Perl Kingsley

I am often asked to describe the experience of raising a child with a disability - to try to help people who have not shared that unique experience to understand it, to imagine how it would feel. It's like this......

When you're going to have a baby, it's like planning a fabulous vacation trip - to Italy. You buy a bunch of guidebooks and make your wonderful plans. The Coliseum. The Michelangelo David. The gondolas in Venice. You may learn some handy phrases in Italian. It's all very exciting.

After months of eager anticipation, the day finally arrives. You pack your bags and off you go. Several hours later, the plane lands. The stewardess comes in and says, "Welcome to Holland."

"Holland?!?" you say. "What do you mean Holland?? I signed up for Italy! I'm supposed to be in Italy. All my life I've dreamed of going to Italy."

But there's been a change in the flight plan. They've landed in Holland and there you must stay.

The important thing is that they haven't taken you to a horrible, disgusting, filthy place, full of pestilence, famine and disease. It's just a different place.

So you must go out and buy new guidebooks. And you must learn a whole new language. And you will meet a whole new group of people you would never have met.

It's just a different place. It's slower-paced than Italy, less flashy than Italy. But after you've been there for a while and you catch your breath, you look around.... and you begin to notice that Holland has windmills....and Holland has tulips. Holland even has Rembrandts.

But everyone you know is busy coming and going from Italy... and they're all bragging about what a wonderful time they had there. And for the rest of your life, you will say "Yes, that's where I was supposed to go. That's what I had planned."

And the pain of that will never, ever, ever, ever go away... because the loss of that dream is a very very significant loss.

But... if you spend your life mourning the fact that you didn't get to Italy, you may never be free to enjoy the very special, the very lovely things ... about Holland.

Positives Out Of Perceived Negatives

I never 'planned' on having a Neurodiverse child, but you parent the child you've got, not the one you'd have liked to have had. I don't view my child as disabled, he simply has a different brain wiring and it is up to me, as his mother, to accept that child and love him and do as much for him as I do for his Neurotypical brother. I want them both to be happy, healthy (mentally and physically), and productive members of society. I want them to be accepted for who they are, whoever they are, and if you must apply a label (and they do have their uses), whatever they are.

I have never seen my son's diagnosis as a disability. I have never seen it as a burden. As far as I can tell, neither does my son. It is simply a part of him. I have always been a person who will look to find a positive in any given situation. It took a lot of work, tears, stress, exhaustion and frustration, but I believe that I can show others that Neurodiversity is not a negative. It can be a huge, massive positive, that simply requires acceptance by one and all, with adjustments being made by the Neurotypicals, who find change easier far to manage. If I can do that, then I've found my reason for being on this planet!

Me receiving a Police Commendation from Assistant Chief Constable Dan Vajzovick in July 2022. He was the senior Police Officer I made the original suggestion to in February 2021. He had been incredibly supportive of the Supported Internship Scheme that I set up, right from the beginning to the current time.

Noor Ashikin's bio

Shikin is a firm ⬛⬛⬛ pose in life and building relationships with others, Noor Ashikin is a mother of 3 wonderful boys. Her life motto is "work-life balance is key to being successful mother and valuable relationships". She believes the need to self-care in creating meaningful relationships. She is active in the Toastmasters movement having been President of Singapore's bilingual Malay-English club; the Jauhari Toastmasters Club. Shikin is in her first year of a Master's Degree in Counselling and Guidance.

Shikin writes in flawless Singaporean English.

Her Instagram is https://instagram.com/simplyhappy_kin?igshid=MjAx ZDBhZDhlNA==

Chapter Five

Self-Care, A Social Life And Self-Development Are Crucial Especially For ND Parents

By Noor Ashikin Binte Shahirudin

This chapter was written in the hope that all parents, particularly mothers with special needs children, will take good care of yourself first in any situations. In most situations, we believe that as parents, we put children first before ourselves. This is usually the case when circumstances do not allow us to have room for negotiation. Traditionally, our preconceived notions of babysitting our children are not easily erased. When it comes to children, we often neglect the need to be healthy not only physically but most important, mentally and emotionally. Most of the time, parents, particularly mothers, are drained where babysitting children is concerned. The repercussion of neglecting our own health is negative. How many of us are caught in situation where we rant at our spouses and children or fall into depression when we are so drained? Please know that you are not alone.

It was clear that my first-born child was special and extraordinary by the symptoms he exhibited. He was extraordinary in his non-verbal communication. He was special in his own ways. He responded to our close ended questions, yet he demanded small requests requiring two or three sentences. When he was diagnosed with autism spectrum disorder (ASD), my life felt empty. Based on *Diagnostic and Statistical Manual of Mental Disorders* (DSM-5), a guide created by the American Psychiatric Association that health care providers use for diagnosing, people with ASD often faced difficulty with communication and interaction with other people. They often have restricted interests and repetitive behaviors. I was lost. The only thing I knew was to save him as much as I could, as his mother. He was my priority in whatever I did.

I read books on ASD to equip myself better in parenting him and began my journey of enrolling my special child with speech therapies that he deserved. I dedicated two whole years just to be with him right after he turned 6 months. In these two years, I learned the meaning of patience, faith and hope. While I was so engrossed chaperoning him in all the speech therapies, I neglected my own mental health. I gave my all to him. Just like all mothers will do, I prepared his meals and packed for him when we go outside. I did marketing for the freshest food for him in the hope that he grows up healthily. My intentions just like any other mothers, was pure and sincere. Giving my best for him was the only goal I had in mind. This means that even if I have to lose my savings or be separated with others, I would for his sake. My job at home during the two years basically evolved around him. The decisions I made was all for his best, and not for myself. During those two years, I wanted to further my studies, learning that there was opportunity, but I gave up. In my mind, I was thinking if I were to leave him under the care of my parents or in laws, it would not be the same as I did. I was disappointed in myself that I gave up that learning opportunity. Deep down in my heart, I knew that my child needs me more. However, I made the mistake believing that only I could handle him and no one else could. This mistake took a toll on me. I was emotionally drained. In those two years, as a mother who stayed home, I made so many sacrifices that burned me out. I ensured that food was always on the table, clothes were washed clean and neatly folded and home was in good care. I neglected myself totally. When I looked at my reflections, I was staring at a haggard looking mother through the mirror whose soul was lifeless. The calls I made to my parents were cries for help. Whenever I called them, I felt better, and they reached out to me. I really treasured those times when my parents in law visited me twice a week to play with my child. I took restful breaks taking short afternoon naps or reading book whenever they came by. When I felt better, I called my friends to ask how they were. As my friends were working on weekdays, the void in me never went away. Unlike me, my girlfriends were busy working, some were dating, and some were juggling their motherhood duties while working. I realized that I was alone in raising my child most of the time, given my partner's unpredictable working hours. The weekdays at home with my child seemed longer as I was alone with him. I felt drained, empty and lifeless while waiting for the weekends to cheer me up. The motherhood journey was not easy. It was not one without doubts. I had doubts about raising the special child for the very first time. I took the blame upon myself when things did not work out the way it should. I read and often got myself more worried with the answers I got. For example, whether

I should give my child a specific consequence to his undesirable behaviour, was daunting me. In those two years of parenting, I doubted my parenting skills. As I believed that I was the mother who knew best, I corrected my parents or in laws of how parenting the special child should be. There was no definite answer to my questions or their questions either.

In the arduous journey of motherhood, fortunately, I made friendships with my neighbor who is a stay home mum. When we have completed our housework, we took a short walk with our children in the neighbourhood. I counted my blessings to have her support. We shared recipes and from there, I enjoyed cooking. In times like this, having a friend staying right beside me, helped with the emotional distress. I find joy in my reflections I shared with her, and together, we recharge in the things we did such as cooking, walking around our neighbourhood and engaging deep heart to heart conversations. At least, with my neighbour around, I did not feel guilty of spending less time with my special one. I could still do the things I enjoyed doing with my special one beside me. The issue I have is always with myself. I have always felt guilty and doubtful of others taking care of my child when I am away from him. The guilt arrives when I feel bad leaving him who needs so much attention. As a mother of a special one, I did not feel good when I am not by his side. It seemed that the bond I had with him was so strong that I could not bear myself leaving him for my own self-care. I will be engulfed with doubtful questions about leaving him in the care of my parents or in laws because many negative thoughts will run in my mind such as "can they handle him?", "will he behave?", "what if something bad happens?", "I will never forgive myself for leaving him.". I have neglected my own mental health because I was battling with myself.

The battle was real and each time, my friends called me to ask me out, I would hesitantly decline. Unknowingly, refraining myself from meeting others has negative effects on my relationship with my husband. I feel emotionally stressed, and sometimes overwhelmed, when I must manage my special child alone when he went to work. The issue I had in my mind was bothering me. Why should I be the one doing this alone most of the time, when he could go to work and meet friends on weekends and enjoy his private moments? My choice of not meeting others was unfair and unkind to myself. Much to my dismay, I wished that I would be in the company of my friends sipping a cup of coffee, chatting and enjoying myself like I used to be. At times like this, I learned how important support from our close relationships is. In this world, it is impossible to live alone. We need one another. The only consolation I had was hearing their voices over the call and memories came back flashing in my mind those happy moments we used to spend together. Relishing those memories was vivid and happy. Finally at the end of my two years with my special one, I braved myself to ask my husband if I could spend time with my close friends. As I treasure friendships, I did not want to lose my close friends. They were always on my mind and heart. I finally meet them for the first time in two years. Tears of joy rolled down my cheeks as I received the warmest hug from my close friends who have been giving me support through the connections we made via phone calls. This was so meaningful to me. The closeness that I could not describe in words. It felt right to be there at that moment, and I promised myself that I will not allow the opportunities of meeting them slipped away. All this while, much to my resentment, I blamed myself if I were to go out unaccompanied and the fear of being blamed has kept me silent. This was consistent with the traditional notions of mothering (Captain 1989, Swiggart 1991). There was a certain kind of expectations passed down through generations in the Asian culture of mothering, particularly in my family. I would never have imagined breaking away from that cycle.

In the behaviourist view of psychology, mothers are the sources of nurturing the young and protecting them from danger and harm. It is only natural for us to do so. However, we also need to understand that potentially, we become unpredictable mothers when our feelings are overwhelmed and our parenting style is based purely on our mood. If we do not make ourselves happy, the chances of creating problems in our minds, through emotions and relationships, may be passed down to our children inevitably. We need to be mentally and emotionally healthy before we can create healthy relationships with our spouse and children. My mothering experience taught me the re-evaluation of my own attitudes, beliefs and personal characteristics. In caring for myself, I began to pursue the 3Rs which stand for reflections, renegotiation and recharge. Please allow me to share the 3Rs with you. I find meaning in engaging reflections for the experience I went through.

Reflecting on how I respond to situations whether I was with my partner or my special child has helped me to redefine how mothering role should have been. I begin to ask myself questions on how best I imagined the situation to be when I was with my spouse or when I was with my child. I would like my small family to be close knitted and open in our conversations, based on trust. As I reflected on this, I realized the damage I have done to myself all this time when I did not share with my spouse how I feel and what should have been. All this while, I was keeping silent and resented with traditional child rearing beliefs. This leads me to renegotiate on the mothering role. I renegotiated with my spouse on the role I played as mother and involved my spouse in sharing the duties. This renegotiation was done to make him known that I need the self-care I deserved and the positive outcomes it brings when I am mentally and emotionally healthy and positive. The last R I am sharing with you is recharge. All mothers need to recharge to think and act positively. Recharging brings out the best in themselves. Recharging means making connections with their close friends, and relatives. The power of relationships is boundless. When there are no boundaries for self-growth, opportunities and relationships, a person's life is fulfilling. Feeling love and a sense of belonging is essential in making our lives more fulfilled. This is in concordance with Maslow's (1954) hierarchy of needs. Only through love and belonging, mothers will be able to achieve the next ladder of self-actualization which is self-esteem. In my journey of connecting with others, I gained meaning and a sense of purpose in my life.

This has raised my self-esteem when I reflected. I regained the confidence I once had and this makes me contented. I was not tied down with the traditional child rearing beliefs. Feeling accepted opened up my windows to creativity and meaningful life experiences where I started to write my journal and accepted job offer at that time of my life. I went back into the education sector and restarted all over again. There was still fear of being a bad mother by going back to work. However, life experience taught me that I can manage my small family with work life balance if I am able to reflect, renegotiate and recharge whenever I could.

Mandy's bio

Mandy Street is an autistic mum and Speech and Language Therapist in the UK, specialising in working with neurodivergent children and young adults. She qualified from City University, London, with a Distinction in Speech and Language Therapy (PGDip) and works independently and for the NHS. Other careers have included copywriting, waitressing, shopkeeping and unpaid butler (aka parent). She is riding the steep learning curve of collaborative, low-demand parenting, along with her wonderful husband. They neurodiverge around the house with their beautiful autistic daughters, one of whom has a Pathological Demand Avoidance/Pervasive Drive for Autonomy profile. Mandy will talk at great length with you (whether you ask her to or not) about neurodivergence advocacy, autism, anxiety, dogs, frizzy haircare and chocolate. Mandy's Facebook is @MandyStreetSLT

Chapter Six

Autistic Thoughts

By Mandy Street

I'm Mandy, a 42-year-old mum of two lovely girls. I am a Speech and Language Therapist working in the UK, specialising in working with autistic children and young adults (particularly the latter). In January 2023, I got my autism diagnosis and am exploring how this makes me feel, and how it will change my life for the better. Here are my ruminations for Autism Acceptance Week 2023, which I hope very much will inform and reassure other neurodivergent adults. For international readers, my recommendations are all UK-based – however, many are searchable on Google.

Autism And Girls

As I was a girl about 400 years ago and now have two of my own, this is a fab place to start! There is a lot of awareness burgeoning in the media and in the researchers' publications about the discrepancy between males and females with diagnoses. Girls often present very differently to boys for reason that I can't reach for in this little space. Look here for more info:

'Unmasking my Autism' – Christine McGuinness's powerful documentary (BBC Iplayer)

https://www.autism.org.uk/advice-and-guidance/what-is-autism/autistic-women-and-girls -

This is a fabulous, informative, easy-access page on the National Autistic Society website.

When I explain to people that my daughters are autistic, I usually have to explain why – it really surprises people. As my Facebook photos (which tell 0.01% of our actual experience) attest, they can be very smiley and sociable girls. Until that inner anxiety, caused by the perpetual need to please other people and fit in, takes over. Then 'fight, flight, freeze, fawn' kicks in.

Perhaps it's because of society's expectations of them...perhaps it's innate skills that they have driving them to try and interact any way they can... I suspect a mixture of both. However, when we're honest about who we are and how our special brains work, then we can work out what helps us. It's very difficult to do this with autism, as self-reflection is not an easy task, but it is possible. Especially with a) all of the resources out there now and b) a loving and understanding family. How bloody lucky our family are that we have both.

'Standing Up For Myself' by Evaleen Whelton – highly recommended book for autistic young people

'The Secret Life of Rose' by Rose Smitten – written by an 11-year-old autistic girl

https://www.pandasonline.org/ - Neurobears! An online course for autistic kids aged 8-14.

Autism, Anxiety and Masking

I could write about this topic for years and years, because it's huge. And, thankfully, a lot more scientifically-minded people are writing about it too. Masking is a behaviour – essentially changing your behaviour to fit in, mimic or camouflage yourself amongst others in order to feel accepted and to fit in.

I can't apologise for being over-dramatic in the face of facts: I'll directly quote Dr Hannah Belcher from the NAS website: "Studies are now beginning to find how detrimental to our mental health masking can be (Bradley et al., 2021; Hull et al., 2019). Autistic people who mask more show more signs of anxiety and depression, and the strategy may even been linked to an increase in suicidal behaviours (Cassidy et al. 2018)."

There is a real and significant and complex relationship between autism and anxiety. This is true for both boys and girls, although girls are notorious for their masking. All humans mask, in order to interact with those around us. However, this is a problem for autistic people, as autistic social 'norms' are so different to society norms. Masking takes a lot of energy, and it detracts from your own real identity. What is especially damaging, is that young autistic kids don't wake up in the morning and think 'I must mask today'. They do it inherently and automatically as they try to weave their way through a world that is not designed for their sensory, processing and social needs. Not to mention school and social environments where kids can be conditioned to think 'I must fit in' in order to be happy.

Hence, anxiety. When you're using all your energy to communicate, fit in, connect with those around you, then even those with dear and loving friendships are exhausted, every single day. Even if you're fortunate enough to be held by some proper understanding and caring folk, then the environments and expectations of work, school, shops, shows, public transport can be so draining as you try and navigate them and not 'stand out'. All this stress can easily lead to autistic burnout, which is another rabbit-hole you can fall down in all the autism resources – it is extremely real and wholly draining.

Again, it's essential for kids to hear from a young age that their autistic minds are not broken or inferior to neurotypical minds. They are different, and any difficulties they face are not because of them doing anything wrong – it's because the world, and society, and all the places we have to be, are designed for neurotypical people. It's ok to feel stressed and it's always ALWAYS ok to take a break – an autistic person is likely to need a lot more of those! Again, young autistic kids really struggle to reflect on their emotions and why they're feeling them, and to problem-solve when they're feeling very heightened. Supporting them is much more challenging – but flippin' rewarding when it works.

Infodump

https://www.mind.org.uk/for-young-people/how-to-get-help-and-support/

The fabulous work of Sally Cat, an autistic adult with PDA. Here are some of her great masking memes: http://www.sallycatpda.co.uk/p/memes-about-masking.html

https://www.autisticrealms.com/post/supporting-children-through-autistic-burnout-parents-guide – guidance for parents on supporting kids with autistic burnout.

Books

'How The World Isn't Built For Autistic People And What We Should All Do About It: Untypical' by Pete Wharmby (Harper Collins, 2023)

'Different, Not Less' by Chloe Hayden, a young autistic author (Murdoch Books, 2023)

+ a million more books recommended to me by people recently which all look great.

Autism And Education

Hello! Me again. Before I start blathering on about education, I'm going to start with a disclaimer: I know so many teachers and there is not a single one that doesn't devote every last grain of energy to their overwhelmingly demanding job. This chapter is not about teachers failing. And if I mention that sometimes there is less awareness of certain needs at school, it is not because the teachers don't desperately want to know more about and support all the children in their care.

I mentioned in my post on Autism and Masking that society is not designed for neurodivergent people. This is why, in some ways, autism can be said to be an impairment. And it is why, in my training as a speech and language therapist, and in special educational needs training throughout recent history, autism is described in terms of what 'difficulties' a child has. These 'difficulties' tend to be framed as what the child isn't able to do. For example, they don't make eye contact, they don't take turns in conversations, they don't perceive what other people are thinking.

In other words, they don't act like neurotypical people. Which of course they don't. Because, um, they aren't! It's only recently that I've become very happily aware of neurodiversity-affirming ways of working which mean that I can now work with a child on their communication without trying to train them to make more eye contact, force them to interact in ways which really stress them out or expect them to work incredibly hard to see someone else's point of view without learning to advocate for their own.

On one level, autistic people have to find a way to live comfortably in society. On another level, there is massive work to be done on helping society adapt, accept and appreciate autistic people and the way they communicate. We can't change society overnight, but I think by reframing the work I do with each autistic child, they can learn to tell neurotypical people what they are like, and what they need from the neurotypical person. This is also a hard goal – that difficulty in reflecting on what you are like, how you feel and what you need is very real. However, the teenagers I'm working with are hugely eloquent about what helps them when they're communicating.

The heartbreaking thing is that they don't feel they are in the right. They feel they get things wrong, that it's too difficult communicating, and they want the rest of the world to know how hard it is. And why should the autistic kids be doing all the work?

In our experience with our littlest girl not being able to go to school, as the overwhelm, anxiety and stress just got too much, the pressure was immediately on her to try really hard, push through the difficulty, get back into the place that was distressing her so much. She needed loads of time – more than the constricted school system could allow – to recover from burnout, develop rapport with new teaching staff and build trust that she would have that time, space and flexibility at school. But what mainstream school staff can realistically provide those three things with their current incredible funding and resource constraints? It is more cost-effective to get children to follow one set of expectations – attend school, wear uniform, follow the timetable, comply with the curriculum, organise yourself from Key Stage 2 onwards etc.

But autistic children (and many other neurotypes...and indeed many neurotypical personalities) cannot do these things. Their processing speed, emotional and sensory regulation requirements, communication styles and executive functioning abilities, mean that they just...can't.

I know that saying state education is 'one size fits all' is generalising, and not acknowledging the hundreds of schools and state provisions working hard to adapt, integrate and support their struggling children. However, the basic educational tenets of this country are one size fits all. This does not work for autistic children. An amazing specialist autism teacher shared a picture with me, with a chicken on stilts, walking around with some flamingos.

Help the chicken develop its chickenness. Stop expecting it to be a flamingo.

Resources from people who know more than me:

https://salvesen-research.ed.ac.uk/leans - a free programme to introduce mainstream primary pupils aged 8-11 to the concept of neurodiversity (UK based) http://tinyurl.com/yc62csmz - A conversation starter comic strip to talk to neurodivergent kids about what they might need

https://icannetwork.online/online-resources/ - LOADS of stuff from Speech and Language UK (formerly ICAN) about settling into secondary school and a squillion other good things for kids to explore their brains!

PDA

This will be a little more personal because we've recently realised we've been living with this complex profile of autism for several years, in the form of an exceptional and beautiful little person! When our lovely oldest was diagnosed I was as confident as a smug professional who works with autistic kids could be – I knew something about autism and girls, masking and anxiety, and we were so fortunate to have a paediatrician who knew it all too. The whole assessment process was like a supportive conversation. Our oldest was quite excited to learn about it herself, although the reality of navigating autistic adolescence is only now becoming apparent (maybe I'll rant about that another day).

Our littlest daughter is autistic with a Pathological Demand Avoidance profile. I deep-dived into this in autumn last year, after reading a blog post by the AMAZING mummy at Steph's Two Girls and I had a massive lightbulb moment. It is concisely summarised in another Sally Cat meme (attached), which touches on the fact that it's not actually recognised as a 'medical diagnosis' as autism is. A clever and canny paediatrician will get round this by describing it in a myriad of different ways (thank goodness).

I think of our daughter as existing in a permanent state of 'fight, flight, freeze, fawn' – the instinctive responses of our amygdala (primal monkey brain) to danger. She is hyper-vigilant and always on the watch for what demands a situation, person or event might bring. Demands ignite her nervous system to the extent that severe anxiety can kick in extremely quickly.

It's thought to be a profile of autism, as there are some of the differences in social communication, sensory processing and super-focus on interests that are prevalent in that neurotype. My goodness though, I had 'just' thought that she was very anxious – I had no idea until the middle of last year that she might be autistic too. Now that she has unmasked a bit (which is better for her), she can't do the eye contact or reciprocal conversation that some neurotypical people can, she has a lot of sensory needs (perhaps another blog post needed there too?! Argh! I'm never going to shut up!), and yes – it all makes sense.

Some PDA-ers prefer the term Pervasive Drive for Autonomy, which describes the person's need to maintain control over a situation. When the situation becomes unpredictable or they feel it is out of their hands, the anxiety can be overwhelming. People with PDA can be championship maskers (if only it were an Olympic event – we'd have a cabinet full of medals!), and will often use social strategies to cover their anxiety. For example, our lovely girl will divert our attention in a demanding situation, deflect questions and instructions, change the subject, or (and this is fawning) smile and fit in.

And the thing that is so so hard for her – this happens with nice 'demands' too! She has missed birthday parties, family gatherings, trips to places she actively wants to because she can't stand the pressure of expecting to enjoy it or knowing others want her to enjoy it. She will become wound up, oppositional, stressed, distressed and at the worst has a meltdown. And a meltdown is not a tantrum (which typically describes a behavioural response). It's a full-on anxiety attack – physical, verbal, emotional. We tried describing them to school and they just couldn't accept that these were reactions that couldn't be tamed with appropriate parenting. They're exhausting to experience and she needs a lot of time to recover from them.

Thank GOODNESS for the PDA society and for amazing bloggers, such as Steph's Two Girls, Missing the Mark, Dr Naomi Fisher, PDA Our Way and the incredible resources at Not Fine At School's website. We are now low-demand parenting, she is given a lot of control over her environment, and her mental health is slowly recovering. She also knows about her diagnosis, and there are further resources to explore it when she is ready. It's a huge leap of faith – as parents we're told we must be in charge, instruct, stipulate, encourage, coax etc. You tell people that you are now suggesting, commenting, collaborating, strewing information around for her to access in her own time (if she is motivated) and they are quite likely to laugh in your face or advise you to go on a parenting course.

But she is feeling better, and is gradually doing it all at her own pace. Now we have medical bits of paper to back up what we already bloody knew, some doors have opened for alternative ways of educating which we're really excited about.

I know COVID did a number on loads of children's mental health, and it certainly exacerbated Ivy's situation. But the system that is trying to educate and streamline all our diverse children has not helped either. I never thought I'd become a confrontational asshole…but I shall be learning to be one to get what she needs. (Well, a very polite confrontational asshole). (Although I have shouted in a meeting now, which was very refreshing).

At the start of the school year, a member of staff at school did some reading up on PDA and saw the strategies and approaches that are recommended by parents of children with PDA (and by adult PDA-ers themselves). She said 'it sounds like a lot of hard work – I don't know if you'll want to go into that'. But it's not a choice. We saw what persistent demands were doing to her mental health. And now that she has had some little time to recover, and we have started to provide the environment she needs at home, then things are improving for her. When your child is struggling of course you provide them with what they need!

https://www.pdasociety.org.uk/
https://notfineinschool.co.uk/
'The Panda on PDA' by Gloria Dura-Vila (Jessica Kingsley Publishers, 2022)– a lovely kids' book about PDA
'Can I Tell You About Pathological Demand Avoidance Syndrome?' By Ruth Fidler and Phil

Christie (Jessican Kingsley Publishers, 2015) –
another great book

'Your Child Is Not Broken' by Heidi Mavir
(Authors and Co, 2022) – just brilliant must-read for
parents of neurodivergent children.

Autism And Me!

In January this year, I got my autism diagnosis.
Writing this makes me smile, which is nice! Telling
people does make me want to hide in the cupboard
under the stairs, though. Basically, the things I've
written about in my Autism Acceptance posts play
such an intrinsic role in my family because they are
relevant to my kiddies, but also because they are
relevant to me. I'm not going to write my biography,
but I wanted to share a couple of ramblings.

I'm actually feeling like such a newbie, as the
mask that I wear has developed and changed – only
slipping once or twice – over so many years that it's
now really ingrained. I don't really know who is
Masked Me and who is Unmasked Me. Following the
advice of the beautiful little illustrations at Autism
Happy Place, I will try lots of things until I find out
what is comfortable!

The hardest thing will be asking for
accommodations that I am convinced to my core I
don't deserve. I suspect it may be quite
commonplace that along with a late autism diagnosis
comes a healthy co-occurring dose of Imposter
Syndrome. I absolutely can't believe that everyone
else doesn't experience the world in the same way
as me (which, um, is actually quite autistic of me),
but they generally just cope with it better because

they are Superior Humans. And it is such a struggle to write these words without constant jokes and disclaimers about how 'everyone gets tired of course' and 'parenting is a bit of a shock to most people' and 'we all get a bit more set in our ways as we get older'. Well, there – I just made them anyway, as I think they are true. But there is definitely something else going on in my brain which affects the way I process things.

Anyway, the lovely clinical psychologist who diagnosed me sent me some very super diagnosis paperwork, including a run-through of how I map on to the autism diagnostic framework. It's quite an interesting framework anyway so I will share a bit...

Reciprocal communication (small talk, back and forth, starting and carrying on interactions etc.) – I've learnt to do so much, and I think it takes me more effort than I realise. I believe I'm quite good at it now. Any struggles I have aren't because I'm not interested in the person I'm with – I'm just a bit clueless about how to make that leap into conversing. If conversation flows easily, it's because the person I'm with is a really good open communicator – so well done, friends who have conversed with me! You win, and thank you!

I also use humour to participate in interactions – sometimes even successfully!

Non-verbal communication (eye contact, facial expression etc.) – I thought everyone counted while they make eye contact and felt gut-wrenching relief when they didn't have to make it? Again though, I'm so used to it now that I can do it instinctively without wanting to run away – but every time I make it, I notice.

Developing and maintaining friendships – I do not know what the HECK I would do without my friends. I have two absolute essential core friends whom I've had since I was very small and another little collection of long-term 'keepers'. There must be something about them, as communicating with them is such a pleasure – I think I must unmask with them a bit (usually stuttering away and forgetting what I'm talking about, which I can now hide behind peri-menopause lolz).

But it was SO VERY HARD when I was younger. I tried to get everyone to like me and I still have an absolute horror of not fitting in. I've become a veracious people-pleaser and I get so anxious about confrontations. Having children has made me a little more confident about that though – I will bellow at anyone who challenges them. I have so much to say on this – maybe I'll do some more posts one day.

Repetitive movements and routines – oh, hair-fiddling, face picking, slightly odd eye movements, and just try changing my plans and expectations at the last minute. No, actually, please don't!

Particular focused interests – there have been loads, and I suspect my current one may be autism!

Sensory issues – I'm trying to reduce my word count now, so let's summarise. Eating noises, bright lights, people touching me, labels in clothing, and a few more.

There's a lot more in the documentation, and what I'm doing now is finding out that I actually deserve to have some accommodations made for me. I absolutely hate acknowledging that I deserve positive attention or assistance so this is a huge step.

Again, there are resources galore which is so amazing – and a lot more awareness in the media.

I am so fortunate – I have my lovely family, a job I like (now I organise it all on my terms) and the most wonderful supportive friends. I am bloody exhausted though, and my teenage years were ever so much not fun. I now really really want to support other young people to find out about their own personal brand of autism and what sort of help they deserve from the rest of the world. Because they are all working very very hard, and they all deserve that help.

Useful things:

Again, 'Unmasking My Autism' – documentary by Christine McGuinness.

'What I Mean When I Say I'm Autistic' by Annie Kotowicz (Neurobeautiful, 2022) – superb book

https://www.autism.org.uk/advice-and-guidance/topics/diagnosis/diagnostic-assessment/adults

https://www.facebook.com/groups/autisticparentsukpeersupport/ - wonderful group for autistic parents in the UK

All my family and friends – best resource ever!

Carolyn's Writer's Profile

See my Amazon Author Central page for all the books I have worked on.
https://amzn.to/3KxZmWY

Carolyn - the, Erstwhile 'I Talk, Not Write, Not Ever' Person.

But things can change. Passion Plus Purpose Trump Personal Protests and Ph.E.A.R.S*. (Fears are just Phobias, Expired Experiences, Aversions, Resistances and the Startles Of Life, see 'Fear & Us'.

In terms of writing and writing as a person of credibility and authority, Amina Lucas has Carolyn's eternal thanks and hearts for the encouragement to be a writer.

Carolyn's first published piece was as a contributor to the book 'Speaking In Public' authored by Amina (see my Amazon Central, link above).

Carolyn was Head of Public Speaking for ten years at a Polytechnic where it was a module of student's choice. Amina, still a great friend, joined the teaching team and the rest is history.

We wanted a book our Singaporean students could relate to. All of the previous versions of the subject had textbooks from the UK and US tailored to students of Universities from different cultures. Aside - due to the terms of her contract, Carolyn was unable to be listed as co-author.

Carolyn plans to do a solo authority guidebook on Public Speaking when the whim takes her.

You Knew There Was A 'Ah But' Backstory Coming, Right?'

Attributing her difficulties to what she knows now are aphantasia and ADHD with dyspraxia, Carolyn dreaded every single writing assignment throughout school and University. At Prep School there was a letter-writing period every Tuesday after breakfast and even the eleven-year old her couldn't get her mind to start its engine.

As for journalling, Carolyn has this to say. "Journal your thoughts - they all push penning down whatever one has in mind, All the time. My thoughts don't make it to pen let alone to paper. Not 'on commando!' To my mouth as spoken words? Like a boss.*"

She loved 'The Artist's Way' however some approaches cause more harm than good, despite what the fans say. A neurodiverse person feels defeat and like a failure with many of the approaches loved and held sacrosanct by others.

She now knows that she can write but the topic has to be something close to her heart.

And not everyone is in a person's real audience.

Spot the neurodivergent. She was always on extensions and extensions of extended deadlines. Every essay came back 'great ideas' and 'well done' but 'LATE', disorganised', 'messy', and often 'hard to follow' with question marks all over, albeit not in red as was the ethos of the school. Thank goodness for the tech that enables us to move bits of text around.

Her final paper for her Social Policy Bachelor's degree ended with the question 'What Is Normal?'. Needless to say I could have talked the hind leg off Donkey Kong on that topic. But would the same thoughts exit my brain onto the answer sheet? Not that day.

So now you know. Carolyn's 'why' for writing is to get her work and the contents of her genius brilliant mind (we each have one) out to the folks who are her audience and have similar dreams of enabling others to write their truths both for themselves and for those they can and were put on this planet to encourage, be examples for and edify.

TL;DR Carolyn dreaded writing up until that dread was usurped by the urge to enable other aspiring writers and help those living with Life Issues as well as their people and the professionals who are neurotypical. Like André the psychiatrist who diagnosed Carolyn with ADH- little d.

Moral of Carolyn's every story: Passion Plus Purpose Trump Personal Protests (in these ten seconds).

PS according to Oxford Languages and Carolyn's favourite definition,".

Chapter Seven

By Carolyn Street

This Chapter has four title options:

One Whose ADHD Is It Anyway?
Two My Takes On ADHD as an as a multi-niche, ADHD-tastic psychotherapist, coach and public speaking and writing trainer and mentor and French and German language teacher, translator and tour guide.
Three The Gift of Being Able to Think One Thing While Presenting A Whole 'nother Thing And Other So-called 'SuperPowers'
And my favourite
Four Navel-gazing? Guilty! But for a good cause.*

And with that said - hello! The purpose of this chapter is to share some of my experiences with clients who are on one spectrum or another.

One of the questions constantly taking up my headspace is 'whose attention deficit is it?'. The vignettes below are part sharing and partly a task for you to see who in the scenario is attention deficit: me, Clovis (let's call George's mum Clovis) and / or George. His name wasn't George but he had a 'Georgey' impact on me.

Non sequitur but anyway... what does 'get to the point!' really mean? For me there are infinite 'points'; or three at least. Our superpower is that we see all of them and because they are interconnected, to speak about one leaves a dearth of key information. That said here comes:

Story One

Lovely 'George'. This is for you and all the kids past, present and future like you. Including my Inner Child.

This happened in early 2020. My consultation room door opened and in bounced 6-year-old George, followed by his mum and Mrs '60PC' who had referred George's 'case' to me. Interesting word, 'case', because it makes the concept all sterile and impersonal. Interacting with ADHD is anything but impersonal. And yes, George's case was all about his ADHD (Attention Deficit Hyperactivity Disorder).

I was sat on the designated therapist's chair by the window, adjacent to the black leather reclining lazyboy (think television chair) in lieu of a therapist's couch. Mrs 60PC had told me that George was uncontrollable and causing problems with misbehaviour and mischief. My mind had done a quick throwback to when I was deemed mischievous and badly behaved. I knew that someone was misinterpreting something and it sure wasn't George.

George bounced to within a foot of me and beamed at me. He then flung himself into the lazyboy and started to wriggle about, singing an original composition of his and smiling as he did. I was delighted, but dreading what would come next. As his mum came in she immediately rushed over to George pulled him to arm's length and in a raised voice said 'Sit properly. Say "good afternoon, Doctor Carolyn" '. I was in the middle of saying 'Hello George, lovely to meet you' and as I finished, he waved, energetically. I told his mum that 'Carolyn' was fine. His face fell as his mum started addressing him.

I waved back and George carried on exploring his surroundings. His mum sat down in the client's chair at the table opposite me. Mrs 60PC reminded me of some details and left.

I gave George some coloured cards and asked him to sort them out in order of his favourites. He started making fans and stacking them up in various configurations. It was so interesting; once he had exhausted all the possibilities he stopped, tried to see if there were any more new ways of sorting the cards. Then he smiled and just waited. A trained trait. Wait; don't make noise or draw attention to yourself. Doesn't matter that every bone in your body is screaming for you to ask for more to do, for some acknowledgement, for anything. He went over to the bookshelf and pulled out a toy which Mrs 60PC reserved for 'playtime'. Surprisingly, his mum said nothing, noting that I was not rebuking George.

Turning to the mum who had started apologising, I listened as she animatedly got one of George's school activity books out of her bag. He had done all of the activities and completed all of the tasks in the book. His writing showed effort but was nigh on illegible to the normal reader's eye. Only a person who used to write like that would have the ability to truly have the attention and discernment and the right squinting skills to apply. I did, being familiar with the excitement and exuberance of the flow when engaged in tasks that make one light up.

I was careful to keep silent, suppressing giggles. I succeeded (years of mastery from practice making better). 'Why you laugh?' his mum noticed my poorly-veiled chuckles in a quizzical way. 'oh nothing - smile - George made me laugh'.

Finally, the mum, Clovis as we will call her, spilled the beans. George's teacher had called Clovis in a passive-aggressive frenzy. Well, in my imagination it was passive- aggressive. George had been told to only do two units. He had done 12 and finished the book.

This had happened a few times and the school 'Were Not Having It'. George was labelled mischievous and maladaptive. Clovis was in self-pity mode. She launched into a whole narrative.

I heard all about how she had done a bunch of community service. Then moved house. She had done all the ducking and diving I mean the whole checklist of what parents here do to get their offspring into prestigious schools.

I wished I had had Tal's chapter to hand but the words that came to mind were a jumble of thoughts. I was overly identifying. I did a quick reframe. I didn't start my woke-educator's spiel about ADHD. I did suggest that the onus was on the teacher to ensure George knew when to stop. Most importantly, the teacher's job was to ensure that he had something to do after completing the 'set' task.

What would you have done? My immediate instinct was to advocate for George. There was a massive gap between his needs and the perceptions of Clovis and Ms 'Teacher-From-We-Will-Turn-Your-Child-Into-An-Automaton School.

Yes, natural tongue-in-cheek humour is a coping mechanism perhaps but it does serve the purpose like 'note-to-self' unspoken irony and irreverent humour are immensely regulating when one needs to be professional.

Knowing that validation of Clovis's experiences was needed - and aware that I must not alienate her for George's sake - I addressed Clovis's concerns. I decided how empathetic I was going to be (as an empath that is not difficult, even though I was professionally opposed to her parenting style).

I reiterated Clovis's concerns to her, so she felt heard and understood. I suggested that in future, she get a second copy of the workbook of the day. That way, George could follow his flow until specifically instructed to do more units... I shared with her that that was my strategy and one I had come up with myself at the age of six or seven. (I told my Dad and he obliged, fortunately).

I asked if she had ideas and she thanked me and asked what I could do to help George at school. Not blurting out 'get him outta there and run!' I gently told her that I would have a word with George, just to try that option out. Hope over experience, after all. I told her my impression of George as a bright, curious and cheerful boy. Her eyes widened as I shared that I was sure he had ample intelligence and a desire to learn, be taught and to interact with the world around him. I then said that there had been a lot of progress made in the field of ADHD. I recounted relevant learning from my time as a trainee teacher in public (state) schools in the UK. I then asked if she could see George as a gifted child. She softened and said 'Yes, actually I love him. It is so so tiring though'. I gave her some coping strategies and suggested Access Bars and Rapid Transformational Therapy for her. As expected she humoured me 'Let me think about it'.

Clovis asked about 'stimming' and how to stop George from fidgeting. It was an embarrassment she said. Stimming or self-stimulation is the tendency to channel 'excess' energy into a repetitive behaviour pattern. George's stim of choice was to sing loudly and make soft sounds like the wind in the trees. I explained this to her and she gave me a blank stare.

I asked if he threw tantrums. No, he was well-behaved in public, she said. For me the energy needs to move and circulate and create ideas and work on my work, such as content like this. However, I am convinced beyond a shadow of a doubt that I and others with neurodiversity (according to the powers that be) have to be seen and heard. For too long we were stifled under the tenets of principles like 'a child should be seen and not heard'. But I digress.

Being a Gemini and genuinely caring about Clovis's perceived challenges, it was easy to do this. Thinking and processing one thing and showing something completely different in ones face, tone and outward behaviour. They call us two-faced but we do it all day 24/7 day in day out just to survive, we neurodivergents of my ilk. Again, many NDs are hardwired to be in the 'differences' comparatives category and die-die must point out the flaws and 'what-ifs'. My response is 'Are you part of the solution or part of the problem?'

Story Two

Very Different Encounters Treating Two 6-year-old 'Autistic' Boys In 2012

Back in 2012 a friend of mine, who did various other modalities, started to specialize in autism. He invited me and another lady, Monisha Assudani who's in the And Us group. Monisha and I have been close since this project. She is Singapore's Access Consciousness Lady and I am such a fan of the Access phrases and body processes.

So I joined them in a project involving two six year old boys. One who lived in Katong and the other one who lived in Pasir Ris. We were to see them once a week and twice every four weeks. So they each had 4 visits per week or so.

We will call the first darling boy Rory. He was a twin, the elder by a few minutes. We will call his twin Romulus. Romulus was evil. Gaaa I cannot unsay that. Interesting point of view. Every chance he got he would do something to make Rory cry or look sad.

His mum told me as I arrived for my first visit that Rory had night terrors and tantrums every night.

I am sharing this because I am sure the home environment affected Rory. There were two large sofas in the living area, open planned with the dining area. One was at right angles to the front door the other one flush against the wall at ninety degrees. Rory was usually with the nanny on the sofa with its back to the dining area. On arrival I would sit on the other sofa and start reading his favourite book about trains to him. He would get up, do a little runaround and dance a bit and play with his train set before joining me.

The first visit Romulus sized me up and asked 'why are your legs so big? you elephant is it?'. He then proceeded to run off with one of Rory's trains.

I realised that the father would tiptoe in, leave the door open and tiptoe his way to the rooms that led off to the side. The nanny told me he did this so that Rory would not see him nor disturb him. The dad would spend time with Romulus doing homework and playing.

Normally nannies sleep with the children or in a room of their own. Rachelle slept in with Rory and the mum slept with Romulus. The dad would spend five minutes every night scolding Rory and trying to motivate him by shouting at him. Whenever I saw the dad he would put his fingers to his lips and go 'shhh' as if I was about to call out to him. Funnies.

During the third visit I witnessed something I wish I could erase. Romulus was making a fuss about his dinner. Mum was berating him saying "why you wanna be like Rory-korkor? Huh?" (korkor means big brother in their dialect). "Korkor not like you you know. Why you eat so slow? Korkor slow because korkor not bright like you."

That is an example of 'Singlish'; the mum was otherwise well-spoken using Singaporean English as it is taught here. Romulus just continued to be

stroppy and sulk. He randomly got up and bashed Rory on the thigh. 'I hate you Korkor I should have mummy to myself'.
The Mum just said "you eat finish we get you Mac's ok?".

Rory was on the sofa by the wall in his usual position just inches away. As usual I was reading to him with the book on a stand and doing Jin Shin Jyutsu holding his shoulder or a finger or toe as he would offer me according to his choice. We hardly spoke. As Romulus bashed him I flinched and Rory grabbed my ring finger. The finger of sadness and also shock. He knew. He stayed like that and every session after he would hold my elbow or a finger. That is what prompted me to do the Jin Shin Duo project where twosomes give and receive from each other instead of one giving or self-help.

The following week the mum told me that since the second session with me, Rory's tantrums had stopped on Wednesday and Thursday nights. I saw him on a Thursday. He would peer over the balcony waiting to see me come out from the carpark to his lift lobby and squeal softly when I appeared. His mum videoed it once. The night terrors didn't stop on the other days until two months into the project.

Rory (not his real name) moved to Australia with his family after the 3-month project because Romulus had been accepted into some special gifted programme of sorts. I hope to this day that the now 11-year-old Rory is healthy and happy.

The Pasir Ris Boy

So to the second boy in the project. The apartment was vibrant, lively, noisy and utterly chaotic to a highly sensitive person. Boys aged 4 - 12 everywhere. I had no clue who were brothers, cousins, neighbours. The first Saturday the mum offered me noise-cancelling headphones. Nothing could have prepared me for the cheery chaos in that moderately-sized flat.

Nizam, the little one who had been diagnosed on the ASD spectrum, took to me after several minutes. He spent the entire time pressing on his iPad to make a dinosaur roar. Halfway through the roar he would press it again. Then copy the sound as if he needed to perfect it. Siti the mum said he had terrible constipation. He would only eat brown rice 'ketupat', a kind of special steamed rice dish that is formed into pillow-like shapes. The other boys left him alone. He was happy for me to do JSJ holding him between the shoulders.

At the end of the three-month project that family also moved to Australia because of opportunities for their three autistic boys (I only knew Nizam) to benefit from the system there.

Mum Siti did a thank you video for us and said that the house was always calm and quiet when I left. (But near insane during - Lol). Truth be told, I stopped needing the headphones after session 3. And the boys started to greet me and have semblances of conversation. What amazed me was when she said that Nizam was always happy and would eat a good meal and poop when I left.

Part Two

Weeks after the projects ended, we the therapists arranged to meet at a restaurant in bustling Little India. I met Monisha for the first time. I had had a really overwhelming day. I had gotten lost and couldn't find the restaurant in the rain. I had had to go back to the car to get my phone which I had forgotten. I was soaked and fraught. Normally I would have settled myself down using the 'big hug', the JSJ remedy for stress; it induces calm and helps one get it together. No time though, as the project leader had come to escort me in. From the proverbial frying pan into the fire. It was ultra busy with customers and staff calling out orders and instructions all higgledy piggledy.

Monisha took one look at me and asked if she could do a clearing. I would have tried anything. She told me to repeat after her 'who does this shivering (the Aircon was on full blast as per usual) and stress belong to?' then 'return to sender with all consciousness attached'. I said it 3 times.

Whoosh!

I was super calm and began to laugh. We all need therapists! We had a lovely evening and Monisha and I are BFFs. I did Access Bars then qualified as a teacher and a few more certifications. I love the Access statements the most.

Monisha can be reached at monishaashok@hotmail.com and her profile on the Access Consciousness website is https://www.accessconsciousness.com/en/public-profiles/monisha-assudani/.

Give what you have. It may be better than you think.

Story Three

Let's call this one Sasha. She was diagnosed with ADHD and was on Ritalin and / or Concerta but let's just say non-compliant. She was very pretty, slim and great to engage with as a client. We clicked easily.

Sasha had been in prison for suspected possession of cannabis, a big deal in Singapore. She had taken other drugs and was dealing with tagging thoughts and memories of the hallucinations. Of being in the classic Chinese version of hell. Of being caught and tortured and devoured by ghosts. She had a terrible fear of the dark. For some reason she would see bats, rats and flying cockroaches everywhere if she went into the kitchen after dark. She would get itches deep under her skin all over. Other hallucinations were too awful to narrate here. I have had some night terrors but dementors and death-eaters are not a patch on her incredibly realistic illusions.

She was so afraid to sleep she would down pints of coffee to avoid falling asleep. Coffee plus meds is a highly risky and totally ill-advised mixture. But her desperation was real.

She was usually too tired for our sessions so I would give her nice meditative hypnotic scenarios. I would hold her outer calf and ankle which is the Jin Shin Jyutsu hold for shocks and deep grief and the impact of memories.

She loved them as they enabled her to switch off the scary imagery and get some rest.

Sasha had been an all A student but had developed anxiety and sleep issues due to stress. She responded well to Rapid Transformational Therapy and Access phrases like 'who does that belong to'? And 'everything is the opposite of what it appears; nothing is the opposite of what it appears'. Her favourite falling asleep technique I taught her was to count backwards from 10,000. I normally drift off when I get to 7 thousand or so; she would last till 5 thousand then konk out. Recently she messaged to say that she had shared the calf and ankle hold with some friends and they wanted to hang out with me. Happy days.

After her second package of four sessions the family went on holiday. She listened to a special recording I made for her with the advice of a few fellow therapists who were more experienced than me. Drugs and their post-withdrawal effects are not visible in Singapore. That is due to the death-penalty still in force here, so they had far better access to information than I did.

Sasha came back a new person complete with a new boyfriend. They had known each other since childhood and the families had travelled together. She told me she was fine and asked to meet for a hot chocolate at her place. We did and she thanked me and said she was fine but would I please treat her brother for his social anxiety. When I arrived for my first session with Sam, her brother, it was after dark and Sasha nonchalantly went to the kitchen to make me a hot chocolate. No cockroaches, no bats, no hell any more. No itches, thank Heavens. Her ADHD was under control and she was on a reasonable dose of meds. Her creativity was no longer hampered. That had been one of her complaints about the previous regime.

With Sam it was a breeze, out of this book's purview. Sasha is still doing really well.
What if we rechristened / renamed / relabelled ADHD as a Wonder. The Wonder of Turbo-Charged Persons with An Insatiable Thirst for Connection, Interaction, Things-to-Do and Learning by Doing, Please Let's Make Something Together-ness". That works for me and my wistful nay wishful-thinking mind in these ten seconds.

What? In These Ten Seconds?

'In these ten seconds' is a tremendous tool for acknowledging ones feelings and states of being. By noticing what is going on once in a while when emotions are fraught and nerves are frayed it helps to check in and gently state what is going on 'in those ten seconds'. The number of seconds is purely arbitrary. They can be minutes or hours. It helps with distractions. For example I was feeling accomplished at having typed out the story of my work with George. That led to me contacting my accountability partner (as is the arrangement) before getting back into flow. Accomplished because I have been working on this chapter in my head for a few years. Not gonna lie. I check in with myself and notice 'I am off-task in these 10 seconds'. In my case I am hyper-aware of the time to the extent that I get nervous if there is no timepiece in my immediate frame of vision. This is a conditioned trait; born from having been a 'fawner' for most of my life. There are so many schools of thought; the most prevalent goes 'there is a time and place for everything'. What if that could take into account the time for inspiration to meet readiness where there is no executive function disorder? Parking that there, to be covered in due course. Scheduled breaks don't help. They are a hindrance when I am in flow and the alarm goes off, putting me out of flow. There is now some mainstream acceptance of this, thanks to authors like Mihaly Csikzentmihalyi.

There are now many Tik Toks and Reels about these things. Everyone and their pet capybara claims to be ND. What's good about that that I'm not getting? Hopefully the powers that be will sit up and pay attention. There is a list of the content-creators I follow in the glossary and resources section. I could tell client stories till Christmas but these are the most poignant and relatable. I have not been able to reach the parents of other kids whose consent I would prefer to have. See my posts in the Facebook group for updates.

Thanks for reading, I hope to have enhanced your understanding and exposure to Neurodiversity with these based-on-true-events stories. Only details that would identify the real persons have been changed. I have their permission to recount the narratives too.

*Snigdha, the neurotypical, rolls her eyes and goes on strike.

Carolyn's Therapist's Profile

Carolyn pursued holistic and energy-based trainings from the earliest opportunity, as she knew her calling was as a therapist, healer and helper. She is now working on the 'And Us' series during a medical sabbatical.

She will resume her practice as the 'Holistic Posy' in October 2023. The 'Holistic Posy', our publisher name (since I took over the publishing with book 7), refers to the healing and therapeutic methods, techniques and modalities Carolyn deploys in a bespoke blend for her clients.

Carolyn sought to find out everything there was to know about healing, as she has had warm loving energy emanating from her hands which she noticed at about age 3. Her uncle pointed it out one day as they were walking to the local shop holding hands.

It was also highlighted by some girls at her primary school when they used to tickle each other's backs sitting cross-legged in assembly. Later at boarding school her dormitory sharers would ask for massages for the same reason.

At about age 7 she realised she was different. See the references to dyspraxia and what she now knows are facets of ADHD.

As you might see echoed in chapters by the other authors, the contents of all her report cards ever went to the tune of "... immense potential. Does not apply herself. Consistently top in spelling, English and Maths. Unable to participate in Physical Education. Doesn't follow Instructions despite her best efforts. Forgetful, disorganised, unmotivated, messy, well-behaved but constantly distracted. Nevertheless she is highly likeable, participative and helpful."

As Carolyn says "inwardly I was so bored after finishing the classwork that I would count syllables in words and do maths in my head. Dad, being a mathematician, always had some maths problem or other for me to be busy with'. Since she discovered JSJ ... "I love Jin Shin Jyutsu partly because it put an end to drawing unwanted attention to myself due to my stimming. I was a horrendous hair twirler and nailbiter; since JSJ it is occasional."

Now I hold my fingers and do JSJ holds or EFT tapping my way; these don't draw attention to me."

Carolyn wants to mention that she failed music theory 5 times between 1986 and 1988 and was unable to take grade 6 flute. She started at age 11 as music lessons were compulsory. It is an instrument she still loves to play at Christmastime. She still strives to sight-read and play by ear. Let's see if she passes grade 5 theory by this time next year LOL. Hold my (root)beer, she says.

She found her zone of genius as a teacher and public speaker. She came top of her class in French the first year at boarding school. Why special? She beat two native speakers of French and true rest of the class who had been learning French for 3 years prior.

Carolyn qualified in 1996 with a Postgraduate Certificate in Education in Modern Foreign Languages. She returned to Singapore for family reasons. She worked as a French and German - English and vice versa translator and PA to the CEO of a German company until joining a polytechnic in 1997. Her post was Lecturer in German and French and Coordinator of their in-house and public foreign language learning programs. In 2007 she was made head of Public Speaking and stayed on for another 10 years.

To this end she holds and provides space for aspiring and accomplished writers to set foot on the first stepping-stones, being published in these anthologies. She also helps people overcome their F.E.A.R.S of being visible to speak in public.

Carolyn is
~ An Advanced Therapist of Rapid Transformational Therapy aka the Marisa Peer Method (2017/18 onwards). Her hypothyroidism markers were in the normal range after the experiment she did using RTT on her thyroid during

the 12 day course. They remain normal to this day. Her astigmatism and eyesight post cataract and capsulotomies improved remarkably too, as her optician can vouch. Weightloss due to surrogate eating was normalised too.

~ A student, self-help teacher and professional practitioner of Jin Shin Jyutsu® aka The Art of the Creator Through Person of Compassion. In August 2023 it will be 20 years since JSJ relieved her of the need for spine surgery at her first 5-day seminar. She also lost 8 pounds just experimenting with JSJ after that first seminar. She is known as the JSJ encyclopaedia of Singapore.

~ a practitioner of Access Bars and Facelift and other body processes.

~ a practitioner of 'Compassion Key' level one since July 2022

~ a newly certified (June 2023) practitioner of Alpha Alignment by Robert Cote.

~ a practitioner and teacher of the Pyramid Heart process handed to her by the originator

~ a Usui Reiki Master (2006) (reiki is too hierarchical and part of the scope of Jin Shin Jyutsu plus anyone can come up with their 'flavour' of it, as she puts it). She does love angelic reiki however, having always believed in her guardian angel.

Carolyn has

Two Master Neurolinguistic Programming certifications, 2006 and circa 2008.

~ 2 qualifications in editing and proofreading though she has had those skills all along. Sadly one needs the certs for the purposes of credibility.

Her Writer's bio is also in the Life Issues Transformed Facebook Group.

Chapter Eight

My Experiences And Inperiences

By Carolyn Street

According to my mum I could recite the alphabet flawlessly at 11 months of age. I learnt to read super early, thanks to my Nan (maternal Grandmother) to whom this book is dedicated. She triggered what I now call my auditastic memory for events, conversations and most things people have shared with me. These I can pull out of my head at will. The official term is 'eidetic' hearing; it is the equivalent of a photographic memory. It has been a Godsend in therapy because I remember things word for word. In Singapore people find it suspicious like I am some spy or something.

I was freakishly good at spelling and remembering and using big words and learning and still am. I was often top in Maths but got bewildered when the alphabet got mixed in, in algebra. I saw things multiple ways and was always made (marked and made to feel) wrong. The reason being the way of showing my 'working'. It didn't match the one true response picked by the teacher. Oftentimes I was aware of what turned out to be the 'right answer' but did not choose to write it down. Nobody took the trouble to investigate. I stumbled over the sequencing required. Sure enough there are now (4 decades later) tonnes of arguments on the web over BODMAS and similar directions. All of which were self-explanatory to me. That is me not seeing another's point of view. Simply put there is no right answer or 'it depends on which method you adopt'. When I got to secondary school in the UK, one of the misnomered 'Public Schools', I excelled at French and German. I found them easy and was ace at learning vocab. On the flip side I fail at other kinds of memory. I have precious little muscle memory and face difficulty sequencing instructions. Much as I love to dance in a group I feel totally klutzy and wrong. Line dancing is fine though the music is not to my taste at all.

A Picture Paints A Thousand Words

But which thousand words? My husband looks at things and takes in the tiniest details. My brother and cousin were able to enjoy the cartoon books depicting the ancient Hindu legends like the Ramayana that my grandmother had stacks of. I gave up on them and took refuge in the encyclopedias. Visual learners are said to be the greatest in proportion. I am auditory and kinesthetic overarched by 'read and write'.

I post what I call 'Public Service Announcements' on social media. At times I share the goings and comings/events in my life with Pulmonary Hypertension. No matter how I much and how carefully I explain that I am fine and not in need of sympathy or the 'care' emoticon; sure enough that is all I get. People look at pictures and assume tragedy. They see text and think 'oh no: so much to read'. TL;DR was made by someone who has a 'normal' attention span, I'll wager.

Why are ADHD people longwinded? Because of what I mentioned above. Everything is (undeniably) connected. Yet we are the ones who are labelled:

Disorganised, Doesn't Apply Herself, Distracted Unmotivated

When I was at school I was constantly grappling with all the trains of thought and possibilities that rushed to mind. Especially when a question was posed, be it a maths problem, a writing prompt or question in class. I often didn't have the resources, means nor know-how to plan my answers. It was also a struggle when I was asked to read aloud in class. The reading material was 'Janet and John' when I was on the Famous Five, Secret Seven, Mallory Towers and The Faraway Tree. I was learning by heart poems like 'Matilda' by Hilaire Belloc, 1870. I remember champing at the bit to get on my way through the Children's Britannica. It was a gift from Dad. I was into some of the Narnia books courtesy of Dad's brother Uncle Norman. I couldn't get into 'Watership Down' for some reason. Nor

'Wind In The Willows'. I was also reading my grandmother's 30 volume collection of another kind of encyclopedia. My brother and cousin were always reading Nan's stash of comic books based on the Ramayana, Bhagavad Gita and other Indian epics.

Pictures Juxtaposed With Text Don't Work For Me - Too 'Busy'

Speech bubbles are confusing (which one do I read first). There is disconnect with who was saying what and the pictures are too complicated and luridly bright. Speaking of luridly bright I would get quasi-traumatised by the Medical journals that would come in the post for mum. She was a practicing doctor who became a highly senior head of research and development. Her career took her to serve as the Chief Executive Officer of a whole section of the Ministry of Health.

'Lest I Digress In Jest Nonetheless'

(I am the quintessential rapper albeit on paper), I will spit it out. It took me what seemed to me to be ages to spit it out aged 6 or so in Ms Lim's class. I was avoidant. For good reason. The task was to read one page from a 'Janet and John' book. Ms Lim was holding said book too near to my face for me to read the large print properly. The text was way too big and blurry. There were three maybe four short sentences for me to read. I could not get the words to come out audibly, though they were perfectly formed. Attempting to read out loud something that I had read to myself seemed an incredibly weird thing to do. I could not see the point of reading aloud the twaddle that was the substance of Janet and John.

There Began My People-Pleasing. People-Appeasing, Fawning. Acting For The Interests Of Others So As To Avoid Being Rejected.

I obligingly produced the requisite sounds after some impatient noises and remarks from Ms Lim, the teacher. Sure enough the other kids called me a showoff and Ms Lim stared and moved to the next kid.

Since my return to Singapore in 1996 till COVID I was a lector at church and had really appreciative feedback.

Anxiety, Object Impermanence, Executive Function Disorder and Sleep-Resistance

I had massive anxiety for most of my life. Remember the part about showing one state when internally a whole 'nother state was in force? That anxiety is or was borne out of attempting to do things as others did them. Trying to plan, for instance. Using a diary or calendar or trying to be 'organised' whatever that really means. Woke folks are now waking up to the fact that noone teaches anyone how to be organised. The word 'organised' baffled me, yet it was a mainstay of my report cards. Please can 'organic' be recognised as an equally good trait.

See 'And Us' book one, 'Anxiety & Us' for more.

Nature or Nurture?

My dad was OCD kind of organised. His vinyl records were immaculately sorted according to some weird-to-me schema. As were the cassettes on which he meticulously recorded the contents of the records. They were all classical music of different genres and I have an adverse reaction to most classical music to this day due to overexposure (my theory).

I have always come across as fun-loving and laissez-faire, easy-going and obliging. That is mainly due in cases where I am depended-upon to be on time. I get a massive rush of bliss and sheer joy built on the relief and feeling of achievement of having reached my destination in time. Especially considering the myriad hells and high waters wild horses and miscellaneous other obstacles. These include the bouts of executive function disorder I 'conquered' on my way from my bed to that moment. The pleasure of no longer (at least until end-of-lesson) being in a quagmire of qualms and questions. A respite from the instances of 'wait what did I just remember that I have now forgotten?'. All quirks of my brain. The pleasure of doing my thing, teaching, facilitating and enabling the students to gain new comfort zones. All this in the spheres of communication. The settings included teaching French pronunciation and German grammar. The role I most loved was helping students express themselves in a mock speech situation.

Object Impermanence
AKA Me The Jammy Dodger

'Jammy Dodgers' is a brand of biscuits in the UK. A person who is a jammy dodger is able to get out of situations most would find themselves not wishing on their worst enemy. True story. I did Classical Civilisation A level. One of the papers was on The Iliad of Homer. In English I hasten to add; I will learn Ancient Greek in one of my lifetimes (in these 10 seconds). I had brought my copy to the waiting area outside the classroom designated as our exam room. My best friend James had asked me to bring my copy so he could check a few things; he was a day pupil and had left his at home. No biggie right? Yes biggie. We had a quick round of testing each other and enjoying the sunshine. Time to go in, a good luck kissyhug. We were very affectionate but totally platonic as James was into other types of humans. I loved him just the way he was. In we went.

It wasn't until I had finished my brilliant (to me) essay on The Iliad that the invigilator stopped at my table while on his second round of the room. I had greeted him as I entered the exam room as he had been my Chemistry teacher. I recalled that it was he who had called me 'clumsy but loveable' many times during his classes 4 years prior.

He picked up my copy of 'The Iliad' and lifted it off my table. Startle reflex, knee-jerk reflex; all of the electricity in the whole county seemed to shoot through me. As a good girl, I didn't interrupt the exam nor flee the scene. I was utterly paralysed throughout the remaining half of the exam time. I had been so hyper focused on getting to my seat. Then came filling in the details on the answer booklet correctly.

Lastly, ensuring I read the questions and interpreted them right. I took care to choose the options carefully. In the process I had totally not realised I was holding the textbook. At some point I had placed it in the upper right hand corner of the - not large - writing desk. Object impermanence and negative hallucination; I could have sworn I didn't see it while it was there in my field of vision that whole time. At dismissal time I went up to the Chemistry teacher now Invigilator and began to tell him what had happened. He interrupted me saying 'Miss Street I know you have not a single minuscule cheating bone in your body. Clumsy yet loveable, yes. With bells on. I will have to tell Mr Weir (the Headmaster) though. You understand, don't you? You and I both know that if you were going to look anything up you would have done so before finishing your essay'.

I was stunned, flooded with gratitude and amazement and completely blur (a local word meaning clueless). The amazing teacher and human had had his eye on me and the book. He had taken extra care to check on my actions. Once I had finished the full essay on the Iliad and not tried to cheat, he planned his moves carefully. He took the book away only after I had finished that question and moved on to the next one. Bless You, Mr Chemistry Teacher! The trouble he was alluding to was the serious consequences of being actually deemed to have cheated in ones A levels. Those consequences entailed complete cancellation of all of the cheater's A level exams. Out of my hands, that.

Soon after that I found out that one of the other students in that classroom doing his exam for a different subject had tried to tell on me. He had tried to alert the invigilator straight after seeing me put the book down on my desk. He raised an official complaint to Mr W but was dismissed, being a known snitch.

I had done the whole sequence of actions absentmindedly. To the majority of people I was confirmed plus chop (indubitably) planning to cheat. Anyway Mr Chemistry Teacher had shushed them. If he had confiscated the book at the start of the exam I would have been unable to write a single word. As it was, my submission was less than half of the questions in the exam as i was unable to even pick up my pen after the book was removed. Just deserts; I got a D for that A level.

I was called to the Headmaster's office a good two weeks later. My exams had ended early and some were ongoing. I hoped for the best but prepared for the worst. I told my mum who said 'How could you be so careless?'. Predictable, bearable.

Mr W was stern but he too knew me as someone ditzy but not a cheater. He looked me in the eye and asked me straight up the key question. 'Carolyn, did you intend to cheat in the ClassCiv exam?' I said 'Mr W I did not.' He nodded and gave me some community service tasks to do. Those tasks meant that I was not able to join in the post A level shenanigans and silliness my peers and loved ones got up to. But I never enjoyed those things anyway. God Bless You, Mr W.

There ends my story on how object impermanence and negative hallucination are real.

Executive Function Disorder deserves a book or anthology of books - on its own. Nothing exists in a vacuum though of course. EFD is like being bamboozled while planning and sequencing basic tasks. My favourite example is getting to the swimming pool; a task which I fail to accomplish on a day to day basis. So I pick a swimsuit, put it on. I find a towel. Put that down, with a note to self to pick it up when I am ready to put all my stuff in a bag. Find a bag. Go to get the sunblock and my towelling gown. Before actually getting them, I remember I lent my goggles to my brother-in-law when he was here pre-Covid (a year pre-Covid was it? Then a good long while while I dither over whether to message my sister to ask her when they last came to visit together). Search for the goggles. Put goggles, towel and the rest of the stuff in the bag. That all takes far longer than it seems. Did I brush my teeth? Check for toothpaste on my toothbrush; if there isn't any I already did my teeth. I don't forget because 'ew' and also I can use that trick because my husband puts the toothpaste on the toothbrush for me. Then a message comes in that I must answer while I am excited by the surprise piece of interaction from the outside world. If I ignore it the person might think I am ill or out of sorts. This is because I always reply straightaway or as soon as I possibly can. That is when my hands are not full or my glasses are missing (another ball game). I take a while to get back into getting ready for the pool. Then the doubts - you washed your hair yesterday, leave it else you will have to wash it after so and so. Oh, now you only have 15 minutes for a swim cos it just occurred to me (brain speaking) oh what was it again? Oh yes, that you have to check on whatever with whomever and they said they would be free until … oh shoots 20 mins from now. Call them or get to the pool? That mental exercise goes on ad infinitum; the decision-making gets overwhelming. I make it to the living room and get ambushed by my dear mum. Mumsy who needs to organise getting to some event with me that is happening in 6 weeks' time and we have to discuss it now.

What would you do? Non-ND folks would have lost the plot (not that there was one) at hello. NDs would be busy relating and be in the middle of their story. To wit - where is your mind now?

Those thought processes are often what keep me awake at night. I lie awake engaged in trying to plan. Despite knowing that there are key elements I would have forgotten about. The experts say 'write it all down' then trust that you will handle it when the time is right; for now sleep is the most important'. All very well but then I have to switch my phone back on. Then turn the wifi back on and wait for the app. Then to make a note and set an alarm knowing full well there are other things I need to take into account but right now have no clue what they were. I usually ask God to remind me; halfway through the prayer I realise I have forgotten what I was asking Him for. My usual go-to is 'what does it take for me to remember that in good time to make sure I do or am what I have promised to where and when I promised to.

Too Much Information - i.e. What Happens When My Mind Isn't Anxious.

Clue: Object Impermanence. It Is Never Just Procrastination (see "And Us' book 2 'Sadness & Us' later).

I missed a major freelance work task not long ago. I am sharing because by the time you read this several months would have passed.

I prepared until 2 am on the Friday morning for a Zoom assignment at 9 am. I made sure I had my visual aids in order. I spent time revising my notes on the previous such tasks I had been involved in.

Sorry I cannot be more explicit; bear with me. Lateral thinking took me to remembering that I had to be up early on Saturday for a community retreat. The start time was the same as the start time of the work appointment the next day (Friday morning in the wee hours but really Thursday night). At that moment I forgot about the work task and a sense of relief came over me. I mistakenly thought 'oh I have to be up early on Saturday; I thought it was Friday but it is not'.

The work task had been whisked away into the 'object impermanence' section of the Tardis of my brain.

I reset the alarm (yes) and missed the work task on Zoom at the appointed hour later that morning (9am). This despite having put it in my scheduler, my reminders and texted my husband who did remind me but I mixed up the 9 am starts and said 'oh it's not till Saturday'. He got confused and, in the process, I fobbed him off. And yes, the rest is history. There is no point crying over the loss of something I now have no control over. To wit: that really worthwhile, thoroughly enjoyable, challenging albeit shoddy-paying work task. Yes, I had a responsibility to be there. I sent an email once I realised the oversight and my muddle. I was sure it has cost me that ad hoc freelance opportunity because reliability and punctuality are valued over ability and skills. Which is fair. I dealt with it by channelling my guilt, desire to just swear at the top of my lungs and anger with some jerky whole-body moves that came organically. I let the sounds out that I wanted to express. I allowed myself to feel the feels 'In those 10 seconds' which is me affirming that something else will come next and I don't need to know what it is. I allowed myself to feel bad and betrayed on behalf of the client.

A friend called and I chose not to tell her about it because her responses would have been too much of a leap from where I was at in my head, heart and gut. I enjoyed the conversation and let it be a respite and a gift. I switched modes and was able to address her topic of the day and continue in a friendly vein. We discussed other projects and ideas we have; some mutual and some just hers.

That is not being two-faced or dishonest. It is the gift of being able to say 'in these 360 seconds I am going to remember that I can be in the moment. I decided not to raise the current issue at hand with the caller knowing that she is so empathetic and kind I would have felt worse'.

After the call I checked back into myself. What needed care, love, harsh words or some good old songs from 'The Head On The Door' and 'Disintegration' by The Cure for self-care? I realised that my entire being wanted Jin Shin Jyutsu love. I instinctively put my hands crisscrossed on my collar bones (clavicles) in a sort of back to front angel wings hold. I strongly recommend it when shocked by something due to ones own mistakes.

I began to chillax immediately. That hold prompts into action a specific group of energy streams. They are the best for adjusting, accepting and adapting to an unforeseen situation or space or paradigm. It was too early for 'At least' platitudes or any kind of reframes. It was too soon for Compassion Key.

I Let Some Crying Happen.
I Grieved My Unbroken Record Of Reliability And My Lost Freelance Work.*

At the time of writing I have not heard back from them, a large Government body, since my emailed apology. There are still some slivers of rejection-sensitive dysphoria. I was sad for a while then all fine. All I can do is pray that the process went fine without me; there have been other instances where I was on standby and not called upon at all. But that is none of my business nor responsibility. And if I start ruminating I will just open the door to alarmist thinking and 'should have/ would have' nonsense. Yes I still feel regret and remorse but talking about it I feel neutral. I am able to tell the tale without associating with it to an extent where I am pulled back into the intensity and drama of it. I do detect some residual shame and annoyance at myself; I will do some EFT tapping once I am done with this for the day. I will show in the Facebook group that accompanies this series. If want to see it, it is under the search term 'Life Issues Transformed And Us' on Facebook. I will do it on Tik Tok too. Carolynstreet5 is my Tik Tok handle or whatever it is called.

What really worked was one of the tenets of RTT i.e. Rapid Transformational Therapy

I love the work, as it enables me to exercise skills I love to put to good use, of which I am sorely lacking the challenge and intrinsic fun of doing. I missed a key opportunity to do that because of a misfire in my brain. Then I remembered one of Marisa Peer's rules of the mind which I realised applies to my situation. In my own words, to fit this narrative I will put it this way.

Your Mind Cannot Exist In Two Camps. It Will Steer Your Behaviour Towards What Is Safe and True For You.

I remembered that I did have strong, deeply ingrained beliefs and attitudes about the actual facts and premises of the work task. That it was against a lot of my strongest values. Most people can say 'It's just a job'. But this one runs deep. Yes I provide a service that is valued by the Government body concerned. Yes, the client was relying on me to be there as I had on other occasions when I performed the task I was due to perform on Friday. My brilliant mind let me get muddled and oversleep because of my own integrity and those deeply held values. Et voilà!

That invariably morphs into 'What am I supporting? This service should not be a thing. Yet I was benefitting from it when I should have stood up for my values and declined the task after the first round when I found out the premises of it. Say no more lest I let some cat out of some bag and this escalates. But by the time this gets into anyone's hands other than the beta readers, I will be well past this issue whether they call me back or not. Phew. Yes my mind served my highest good by 'orchestrating' my absence, masking it as a mixup with the other early start. So I put my palms out facing up to do a process that helps integrate conflicting states and trains of thought.

Question - what values are you repressing as you go about engaging with the world? What values are you demonstrating in your behaviour and attitudes? Are they aligned? Useful here is the Neurolinguistic Programming (NLP) process called 'The Logical Levels'. Some have a longer name for it but that is what it was referred to when I was taught and experientially made my experiences with it.

Limiting beliefs are so badly labelled. Such a convenient term; I doubt half of the coaches and therapists who bandy it about have thought deeply about what those words mean when collocated. Limiting beliefs are a misnomer for when your mind is working with what it knows you hold near and dear. That said, it is important to do the F.E.A.R.S check.

F: Am I afraid of something? Yes, I am afraid they won't call me back and that they will cancel my re-contracting appointment which is set for next week. Can I do anything about it? No I can't; the ball is in their court and I just have to wait. No news is just that. Incidentally they did renew my contract albeit months later, I am updating during final stage pre-upload. Smiley.

E: Are there any Expired Experiences entangled in themselves here? Yes, the old feeling of dread that I will mess up again. All the times when I have bust a gut to turn up somewhere only to get lost because I have no sense of direction and probably forgot to rehearse the route. What can I do? The usual response is 'be careful'. Can I control any more for the next time? Not really. Can I stop it from losing me sleep? That remains to be seen.

A: Am I averse to anything? Yes actually. Averse to the whole rationale behind the task I was supposed to do. To me it is a waste of public resources, indulgent to parties that do not deserve such services. There are far more worthy priorities for Government funds to be allocated to. I could go on but this will suffice

R: Am I resistant to something? Yes. honestly the pay doesn't come close to what the expertise, rigorous training I have undergone, opportunity costs and sheer work is all valued at. I had fooled myself for the longest time. The self-actualisation I derived from doing the work and glee at how it was a serendipitous opportunity. Yes, for the most part my work in this role will be or would be of the greatest value. Someone somewhere is taking advantage of a lot of loopholes and they are being shooed through doors that should be guarded shut. Given how I believe that the work itself is totally anathema to my values, my amazing mind did a good thing.

S: Startle Reflex. The knee-jerk reaction to the message from my mentor caused me to gasp. When we get a fright like that we lose a breath. In that message, she curtly asked me to email an explanation for my absence at the appointed time and Zoom link. That message triggered shock and disbelief. My mind started racing and searching for how to fix it. The timeframe for the work task was well over. I had overslept after going to bed at 4 am having forgotten about the work task because I had conflated it with the event on Saturday. I got into 'professional despite freaking out' mode and emailed a sincere apology. I cited my illness as the reason which is partially true. I did not refer to anything remotely to do with ADHD and what I have typed out here because… sigh. Not my job to wake them up. Besides I had been inexcusably unprofessional to all of their intents and purposes. A case of 'the less said the quicker forgotten', to quote a lovely friend. Truth.

Sleep Resistance

As I type it is nearly 3 am. I didn't sleep in too late and my eyes are getting tired but nowhere near the burning state I often negligently let them get into. I am good for another fifteen minutes.

There we have it; for me and I don't know if I speak for others or not, sleep is a kind of false security. Due to object impermanence and the constant pressure to be on top of everything, we believe we have to milk the time for all it is worth. That in turn disharmonises the Diaphragm Function Energy (motto being 'I Perceive) which protects the heart. A lack of sleep with overwhelming stress and having to overcompensate takes a toll. Presenting oneself inauthentically disharmonises the heart and small intestine function energy. The Leo and Virgo respectively. The motto of Leo is 'I Will' and the motto of Virgo is 'I Analyse'. That and feeling the pressure to conform, just be nice and obey the teacher, not making waves overwhelm that 5th Depth I alluded to earlier. Not to get too astrological here, these are very useful elements in Jin Shin Jyutsu and have helped me immeasurably. I am a Gemini and thus able to be two-faced in a good way. The stomach function energy promotes self-love and self-care. Hence the perception by others that Geminis do not care and are irresponsible or frivolous. The twins are a useful depiction of what I have been talking about. In opposition to that, there is the analysing function of the Small Intestine / Virgo. At surface level it is counterintuitive to the self-forgiving, self-nurturing functions of Gemini. When I got into analysis paralysis about missing the work task, I got into all the negative thinking I outlined above. When I got back into Gemini mode I could practice the rational thinking that is my gift. I could bring in the resources from RTT which helped me understand my brilliant mind and its foibles and be okay.

But back to the subheading of sleep: To keep the Diaphragm function energy in harmony, it is important to observe and be attuned to day and night cycles. See the conflict? If I plan to wake up at silly o'clock which for me is up to 8.30 am, I am invariably in no mind to write or be at all productive. I have totally zero handle on what I wanted to do. There is no remote possibility of getting into any flow. Exercise? I just wrote about Executive Function Disorder at length. That is at its worst at silly o'clock. According to RTT there is an explanation for every state and every behaviour (my words). There are four possibilities. 4 Ps, how convenient even if we have to shoehorn the last one and pretend we have a lisp (funny in those 10 seconds?).

Your mind wants to protect you

Your mind wants to punish you

Or perpetuate what feels good (I made that one up)

Your mind wants to keep you feeling special

The underlying tenet of it all is that the mind does what it thinks you want it to do.

Start a Sleep Hygiene Routine' They Say

Yes, I am guessing that that is easier said than done for more people than I can shake a stick at.

Most people love a routine. My guess is that I was at a boarding school where everything was super regimented. Not at all when compared to some schools but still. Set meal times. Set bedtimes. For me if I stop writing now I will forget what I wanted to say and be unable to write the rest let alone conclude it. Plus it is a pleasure albeit bittersweet. I get to reach into the nooks of my memory to extract the stories, experiences and inperiences to do justice to you the reader. I hope I have done this by thoroughly exploring the supporting information this chapter requires.

Just Let Go, They Say

One point to raise here is that simply 'letting go' is not a responsible nor feasible nor remotely comprehensible thing to do. What does 'Let It Go' even mean? Go where? The adage 'if something leaves you and it comes back it is truly yours' is one I hold on to. My cat is missing; the last time she returned was due to a series of unfathomable 'coincidences' and blessed sheer luck. And the goodwill of someone who is not your typical resident of this city-state. However, I hold the belief that Cue the Cat is safe and no it wasn't my fault. Not entirely. I did notice some odd behaviour and, being in a rush, didn't take measures to make sure she didn't leave the building in a thunderstorm. Ohoh the analysis paralysis and self-doubt are at risk of creeping back in. We have put a line under that, thank you genius mind!

Back to the other cause of sleep-resistance: the awareness of object impermanence and the mindwarps it causes. I do not refer to my mind as a 'monkey' one; that would be both inaccurate a term and an insult to lovely monkeys.

What About The Hyperactivity?

I was very obedient and kept my hyperactivity internalised. I would outwardly present as alert and focused when internally I was entertaining my mind with all sorts of formulaic puzzles. Sometimes it was syllable-counting. At other times, making patterns with imaginary art and craft materials all abstract and other mind-games for fun. I never faked anything until I made it. I didn't fake anything.

One time in my first year at boarding school during a spelling test (as I said earlier I aced at spelling) I had finished early. I blinked and looked up and the teacher called me out for purportedly looking at Red Rebecca's test paper. That was dumb because RR was quick but way slower than me. The teacher did not know me from Adam and was convinced I had cheated. Remember the eye-accessing cues? After I finished the spelling test my eyes went left to access an auditory memory. I realised I had forgotten what time I was due to be picked up that afternoon by my mum's brother who was studying in London and had planned to take me for tea. So my eyes darted to access the recorded phrase where my uncle told me his estimated time of arrival. That time, at age 13, the invigilator was not on my side. She got to know me later and we built a good teacher-student rapport.

How My Diagnosis Came About

I saved this story for last for a reason. I had realised that what I had was ADHD for sure when I read a book called 'You Mean I Am Not Lazy, Stupid or (sic) Crazy? I will check for repetition, taking into account Marisa Peer's reminder that 'repetition is the mother of learning'. Er I can think of one exception and that is repeated stories like my mum is beginning to do. But I digress and that does not impress.

Not that I ever thought I was lazy, stupid nor crazy but I had been on a conscious hunt for why I was different for as long as I could remember. Remember the bit about when 'efforting or trying to conform?' When you are actively presenting one way while your mind is on a completely different train? That has taken a toll on my heart. Yes I was forgetful and still am. I am prone to leaving stuff everywhere. To the extent of leaving cash in the cash machine (hence I hardly use cash now we have internet banking). I inadvertently leave my stuff around, prompting the smartarses to say 'don't you want your stuff / money / jacket / pen / what-have-you'?

I had been referred to the cardiac specialist for the second time. December 2020, just 2 and a quarter years ago nearly. The specialists found nothing wrong with my ticker. This despite worsening palpitations, arrhythmia a a resistance to exercise my whole life. I was talking about ADHD because the conversation flowed in that direction. The specialist said he knew of some connection between ADHD angst and heart issues. He referred me to the psychiatrist, an affable chap called Andre. Andre listened to me for a few minutes and then stopped me. I had explained the real issue and my experiences as thoroughly and engagingly as I could. He stopped me, clearly having done no active listening. He said that I definitely had Attention Deficit Hyperactivity but the last 'd' was a little 'd' not a capital D for Disorder. He pointed to how I had held down a job for twenty years and performed perfectly well (truth; that is how I have to present it) In actual fact as I have stated above it was highly challenging, extra much so because of my ND traits. He did not have awareness of the correlation between the heart and overcompensating and the other terms which I find alien but hey whatever works.

Bless his heart. And that, dear reader, is the story of how I was diagnosed with ADHlittled at age fifty and a half. A complete segue from the purpose of my seeing the consultant in the first place. A fortuitous red herring because I am now able to put a name to what I face as a ND person with the choice to see the good and treat the bad with respect and acknowledgement. And have a container for my experiences and inperiences. That will get old soon, I'll wager. Anyhow.

As it happens I was diagnosed with a scary label (the term we use in Jin Shin Jyutsu to encapsulate those conditions) back in October of 2022, and taken seriously and admitted to hospital. Not to go too graphically into what my everyday life is like, I am now undergoing tests and on medications and so on and so forth - all of which should have happened back in 2016 when I first sought medical aid at the Singapore Heart Centre but there is no point indulging in what ifs, wishful thinking, wistful thinking nor would-have, should-have, could-haves. No regrets they don't work / no regrets they only hurt, as the song goes. In my case it is congenital not idiopathic which mean from birth not of unknown cause. So I was born with it but it is connected to the brain's wiring and that wiring means I get to choose to have fun and I can be a realist and an optimist while being aware of the negative conclusions drawn by some harbingers of bad news.

Glossary And Resources

www.jsj.inc is the official Jin Shin Jyutsu® website.

Article on RTT: bemsreports.org Title Rapid Transformational Therapy (RTT): An Emerging Non-Invasive Therapeutic Modality. Except that RTT is hardly 'emerging'; RTT has won Marisa Peer several awards and accolades.

The Rules of the mind video
https://marisapeer.com/how-to-control-your-thoughts-rules-of-the-mind/

The Scattered Mind (and everything) by Gabor Maté

Anne Maxwell co-authored, with Gary Douglas and Dr. Dain Heer, co-creators of Access Consciousness, the international best selling book, Would You Teach a Fish to Climb a Tree? A Different Take on Kids with ADD, ADHD, OCD and Autism
https://www.blogtalkradio.com/besteveryou/2019/04/04/anne-maxwell--the-best-ever-of-kids-with-add-adhd-ocd-and-autism

The ADHD love couple, authors of "Dirty Laundry" on tiktok and book
https://linktr.ee/dirty_laundry_book?fbclid=PAAaYiX1rdqVMvW8bYQtTSJ__eudiK05vtj9pcc5mcW6ylPUAV24AtmLxTmNo Love them.

All of which is to say that I hope you have found some solidarity, engagement and maybe some entertainment and perhaps a bit of edutainment in this chapter. Be authentic, be you and above all, be the light you were put on this earth to be.

Till the next book or when you show up at the Facebook group (plug, plug),

Lots of love Carolyn

Becky's Bio

Fellow Maltesers and animal lovers please say hello! Much of Becky's bio info is in her fab chapter.

Follow her at:

https://www.facebook.com/becky.jhart.3
https://instagram.com/beckyhart5709

Chapter Nine

My Journey

By Becky Hart

I was born on 23rd December 1996 in Southampton, England.

I am the 3rd child to my parents Sue and Barrie Hart. I have 2 older brothers George the oldest and Edward.

We lived in a small village just outside Southampton called Blackfield on the edge of the New Forest and 1 and a half miles from the nearest beach.

Dad worked during the day and Mum worked part time in the evenings at a Pub restaurant.

By the age of 2 I wasn't walking well and not very verbal.

I had to wear splints to straighten my feet as they curled outwards, I had speech therapy. This helped a lot.

When I was 3 years old we all moved to Leighton Buzzard in Bedfordshire as Dad got a new job.

My earliest memories are of my Grandad (Mum's Father). He looked after me 3 days a week while mum went to work. The other 2 days I spent at a creche. I don't really remember anything about that. I was only about 3 - 4 years old.

Grandad would walk my brothers to school (George and Edward) push me in my pushchair. He would buy a newspaper and Maltesers for me on the way home.

Later at around lunchtime we would go out again to the town and he would get me something to eat. If it was really cold he would buy me chips, they would keep my hands warm while I ate them, tucked up in my pushchair.

These are happy memories that have stuck with me over the years.

The only upsetting thing that I remember is when I was asleep when we got home from school. My brothers would tip my pushchair up and backwards which woke me up and distressed me made me cry and scream.

To this day I cannot bear to be in a dentist chair when it has to be moved to tip you backwards. It must be in the right correct position otherwise I won't sit down on it.

Thankfully I have a very patient dentist.

When I started Primary school I didn't really like it, I missed Grandad. I was assessed in my 1st or 2nd year as it became clear to teaching staff I had a delay in my learning. I was not diagnosed with ASD, but did get extra 1 to 1 tutoring.

In later years I began to get bullied and some of the children would call me names and pull my hair. I regressed into myself. I never told anyone. I now know my anxiety was very high. I had a problem with toileting. I would not ask to go, so I was often wet.

As I moved to Middle school things got worse. The teachers would single me out to answer a question in class and would wait until I answered sometimes several minutes again and my anxiety would go through the roof.

My parents were having real difficulties getting me to school. I would completely shut down and not cooperate.

At 14 years old my Grandad passed away. I couldn't process this and ended up not being able to attend school, the school staff couldn't cope with me.

I became nonverbal and would hide under a blanket if anyone tried to talk to me including my parents.

I had tutors at home for the next 18 months, they didn't connect with me and I would not speak to them.

During this time I was referred to CAMHs (Child and Adolescent Mental Health Service) and was diagnosed with Asperger Syndrome now known as Autism Spectrum Disorder. With these diagnoses I was able to be placed in a school specialising in children with needs, it was here I had a statement to be able to access additional help.

Going to a new school was hard at first. I didn't want to go, because I thought it would be the same as my previous schools. It took quite a while before I got settled. My parents would take me every day for just 1 hour at first and gradually increased the time over a few months.

When I got more settled I started getting school transport again this took a while to settle into. As I had made some friends, one of them got the same bus so with her help and the bus escort was very supportive I managed it in the end.

During my time at Weatherfield Academy (Special Educational School) I slowly learned how to participate and interact in lessons and activities.

I started to connect with other pupils in my class, and learned to start trusting them. I gradually built up a friendship group.

Lessons were easier. There wasn't as much pressure to interact if I felt I couldn't. The school had a small animal section with Rabbits, Ducks, Chickens, Goats and 2 Alpacas.

I really enjoyed those lessons.

My confidence started to grow. I went on an activity trip with school, and did things I didn't think I could do.

I also completed my Bronze Duke of Edinburgh award, it was hard to do but I felt so proud.

In sixth form I started doing work experience at the local college coffee shop and became familiar with the surroundings.

I then spent the next 5 years at college. I achieved a level 1 Childcare certificate as well as basic Maths and English qualifications.

In 2018 my Aunty Denise (mum's sister) passed away. This was a shock to us all as it was quite sudden. With the help of my friends and college tutors I was able to get through the grief much easier than before.

What was supposed to be my last year at college I did a Supported Internship at the local college. I worked as a Receptionist and in Cafe sales. I was doing well then came Covid 19. I had to stay at home and do remote learning.

Because of the break in Education when I got back to college. I got the opportunity to apply for an Internship with Bedfordshire Police.

I think this was a turning point for me. I practised for the interview a lot. I was able to plan my responses. I was so nervous I really thought I would mess it all up.

My Job Coach (Tabitha Ashby) and tutors wouldn't have put me forward for this position if they didn't think I could do it.

I held my nerve, I kept my outward appearance as calm as I could. To my amazement I got the position.

It was at this point I began to believe in myself and abilities. My confidence began to grow.

I did a variety of tasks working with my mentor (Tal Stein) and Job Coach (Lewis Hall) I started in September 2021. My first task was to sort and pack Commemorative Covid Coins. I also did administration work, updated a database, and did some redacting work. I also did a lot of work on the Pegasus Programme which allows people with communication/special needs to access emergency services, I looked round 2 Custody Suites and gave my feedback on them.

I was sad when this all ended. I was invited to Stevenage Police Station to receive a Commendation for my work with the Police Force.

During this time I started volunteering at a local Charity Shop. I was shy and nervous to begin with. I worked at the back of the store labelling clothes, sorting books, putting out stock. As I got more confidence I moved to the front of the shop, now I can use the till and serve customers. I still work there on a Saturday for a few hours.

After College finished I got a part-time job at a local Supermarket. I found this really difficult although I was able to serve customers. I didn't have enough structure and found it hard to approach the managers, just to ask for a break.

My anxiety started to become unmanageable and I was unable to get into work. I reverted back to hiding under a blanket and not communicating. I just couldn't overcome the anxiety.

The managers didn't really understand me.

In the end my Parents just let the managers know I would not be returning to work. I had to leave.

Once I knew I didn't have to go to work I started to feel better.

My recovery was much faster than previous anxiety meltdowns.

At this time I had also interviewed for a position at the Central Bedfordshire Council as a Passenger

Escort on school buses for children with special needs.

Although they offered me a job as relief staff. I didn't hear anything from them for ages. Then in January 2023 I got a call to go in to work for an Induction Day and a trial bus trip. It all went very well, and I was given a few days' work here and there. Gradually I have progressed to more days. At this time I have been working everyday for quite a few weeks. I really like work, I feel I understand the Children as I have been in their situation myself.

At present I am enjoying my job. I have the support I need and get on well with everyone. My manager (Nick Firth) is a great support and makes sure that I am managing well and I have the full support of all the other staff.

I have got other family.

(Dad's family) Nan, Grandpa, Aunties Lisa and Lora live in Cornwall so I don't see them that often.

My Uncle Paul (mum's brother) lives close by. He is funny and makes me laugh.

I have 2 brothers (George) lives in Australia and have not seen him for 5 years. We keep in

contact via video call. (Edward) lives locally. He has just become a dad for the first time. I am now an Aunty.

Also I have got Cousins that I visit.

It has taken a long time for me to realise I am capable of a lot more than I thought I was.

I am looking forward to the future.

Interlude Four - Cuddling

By Stephanie Fam

Interlude Five
Celebrating Neurodiversity:
Welcome to my Normal

By DJ Robinson

As a child before the age of one
I would hold my head sideways to watch videos.
I would push my little fists outward and
backward.
I would make sounds, but have not much affect,
except for my occasional broad grin and
infectious giggle.

As a toddler, I was not walking, talking, going to
the bathroom
like my neurotypical cousin, or other children my
parents had known,
but much like my older brother who had autism.

My big brother and I have similarities
but we are not just alike.
Our sensitivities and communications differ,
but we have similar diagnosis.

I will communicate with you if you listen.
The songs of my videos (my constant
companions)
will tell you how I am feeling or what I want you
to know.

I don't understand people's frustrations
when I don't behave the way they expect I ought.
I don't understand about going to the bathroom,
or not stripping my clothes off
or stealing food from the plates of others
or not wanting to sleep alone
or chewing on things that others deem
inappropriate.

I am a teen now.
I am growing.
I am learning.
I am making friends.
I am loving.
I get frustrated, and angry, and happy and sad
too.

Just please love me
As I love you.

Interlude Six
By DJ Robinson

My older grandson is 20 now, and living in a community living home with other differently abled people. While he is pretty rigid with routine, he talks and even texts on a phone now. He used to have a job, and will probably have one again eventually.

He does use the bathroom.

The thing that amazed me when he was little and as yet non-verbal was that he could read books. He once wanted me to read to him on a visit, and I am thinking I can make the story up by the pictures I'm seeing. He got angry and closed the book. Then he reopened it and pointed to the first word ... 'communication'! If we could only open our minds!

DJ adds: 'Having been a grandma to two grandsons with autism for the past 20+ years, I have learned so much about my own make up, and also that all people have bits of themselves that are different from others. I'm excited to read her (Neurodiversity & Us) when she lands!'

Stop Press! 'I completed my Life Coach training final exam tonight and I passed! SO, just waiting for my e-mail and certificate!!! YAY, I am a certified life coach, at almost 66 years old!' she updates.
DJ can be found in the Facebook group Life Issues Transformed And Us.

Jireh's Bio

Jireh Koh is a polymath and has more accolades and activities he engages in than several of us put together.

He is a multidisciplinary artist, musician, curator and Arts educator whose practice spans across multiple art forms and traditions. In his eclectic practice, Jireh weaves between the disciplines of visual art, music, movement and performance-making, drawing inspiration from diverse fields of knowledge such as medicine, biology, astronomy, psychology, cognitive science, comparative mythology, theology, philosophy and more.

In addition to his wonderful writing skills and self-reflection abilities, he sings in more than four octaves and in various ancient languages. As a musician, he specialises in sacred and folk vocal traditions around the world. His sonic vocabulary ranges from Opera, Early Western church music, Carnatic singing, Hindu and Buddhist mantra chanting, Tibetan and Tuvan throat singing and Nanyin, to name a few. In his sound art and experimental music, he also experiments with technology such as live-looping and cymatics, bringing together the East and the West, the contemporary and the classical.

Jireh has organised and curated multiple intercultural and interdisciplinary Arts and Education projects. He is a recipient of the Ministry of Education's Teaching Scholarship (Overseas) in 2013, and the Outstanding Global Leadership Award in 2023 by ACE International and Edufam International Academy for his intercultural work in the Arts and Education. Through his art and efforts with the community, he hopes to bridge people and practitioners of different traditions, generations and disciplines to foster an environment of inclusivity, collaboration and experimentation.

In his free time, Jireh loves cooking, animals and nature. He is a keen meditator and practitioner of mindfulness, as well as somatic and wisdom-cultivation traditions such as Yoga, Hindu and Buddhist Tantra, Qigong and Taichi.

Chapter Ten

The Hero With A Thousand Masks - A Journey To Integration

By Jireh

The Hero With a Thousand Masks - A Journey to Integration

The Fool
The Prodigal Child
The Competent Masker
The Dark Night of the Soul
The Belly of the Whale
The Taming of the Beast
Awakening to Presence
Awakening to Authenticity
Awakening to Relationship

This chapter expounds on my personal struggles with Autism Spectrum Disorder (ASD) from childhood to adult life. It maps my developmental journey from being (blissfully) unaware of social norms, masking parts of my neuro-diversity after being aware of these norms, to my endeavours at integrating my multidimensional self, including the multiplicity and diversity of masks that I put on.

I also detail the coping strategies I have adopted in order to fit into a neurotypical mould, with some being more sustainable than others. The futility of some of these compensatory tactics eventually compelled me to come to terms with the masked or hidden facets of my psyche.

I mobilise the term 'masking' (also known 'camouflaging', 'compensating' and 'adaptive morphing') here to describe attempts at 'flying under the radar' or 'passing' as neurotypical. I also invoke 'masks' to connote the different kinds of social roles I have to play in everyday life.

Before embarking on my journey to a more integrated sense of self, I will begin by sketching a brief background of where I originally started in my journey.

The Fool
Innocence Is Bliss

I was diagnosed when I was 7 years old, when my form teacher in Primary 1 felt that there was something different about me and asked my parents to take me for a psychiatric evaluation.

I talked to the psychiatrist about dinosaurs non-stop for 2 hours, and was diagnosed with Asperger's Syndrome. The session with him checked quite a few diagnostic criteria for ASD all at once - hyperfocused and specialised interests, and a lack of theory-of-mind and deficits in social awareness.

In the subsequent sections, I will briefly describe the various dimensions of how this cluster of symptoms manifested in my life as a child with ASD.

Theory of Mind

When I was a child, I was told that I did not have what psychologists called a 'theory-of-mind'. Most of my behaviours and worldview as a autistic child purportedly stemmed from this fundamental lack of awareness. Helen Tager-Flusberg, a researcher on ASD, posits that most autistic traits are a manifestation of neurological differences in the experience of realities, selves and relations:

'Autism involves significant difficulties in understanding mental states. The theory-of-mind hypothesis focuses on deficits in reasoning about mental states.". "Evaluating the Theory-of-Mind", A Hypothesis of Autism, Helen Tager-Flusberg, The Boston University School of Medicine.

A simple understanding of 'Theory of Mind' is that people usually have a concept that other people have their own minds with their individual interests and boundaries. People on the spectrum are hypothesised to have a less-developed theory-of-mind.

This meant that I was not aware that other people also have their own likes and dislikes; that not everyone was the same as me or would be interested in the same things as me. In the situation where I talked to my therapist about dinosaurs for 2 hours, I was in my own world. I was also not picking up the social cues that the psychiatrist was bored, uncomfortable or frustrated and would just talk and go on and on without knowing that I have overstayed my welcome.

Interestingly, this very symptom which characterised my ASD, was also the very quality that protected my young self from loneliness and knowing that I was 'different'. I thought that everyone was my friend and didn't know that people thought I was weird or different.

I remember there was this incident when I came home from school during the first week in Primary 1. My mom asked me "How was school, did you make any friends?" I told her, "Everyone is my friend!"

I was literally 'in my own world'.
Oh, how innocence is bliss!

Highly Specific Interests and Over-Sharing

Despite not having a strong theory-of-mind, my young self still had some sense that others were 'people' with thoughts and feelings, and therefore there was possibility of (shared) interest. Which is why I had an overwhelming desire to share (with someone other than myself) about the things that I was passionate and interested about.

Science was an area that I was highly interested in. Thinking that 'everyone is my friend', I would go to school and share my highly specific interests with everyone, declaring to the entire class random scientific trivia like 'HIV is a virus' and 'Mount Everest is the highest mountain'.

My classmates used to call me the 'Mushroom Scientist', as I had a bowl haircut and I looked like a human mushroom, with random facts spouting forth. I remember my one incident, where I came crying to my teacher, because my best friend did not believe me when I corrected him that cancer was not a virus (except for unusual instances such as of H. pylori for Gastric Cancer and Human Papillomavirus (HPV) for Cervical Cancer. But then again, even though these cancers may have a casual relationship with viruses, they are not viruses themselves.) I think my Primary 1 form teacher was a bit amused and puzzled about this behaviour, which led him to contact my parents to get me checked.

I was a voracious reader, and finished reading 2 whole sets of encyclopedias by the time I was 7. In particular, the dinosaurs and outer-space ones were read so many times front-to-back that the spines were torn and falling out. I then started reading Medical journals at 8 as I was fascinated with Biology, the human body, the natural world and the invisible microscopic world. I would roam my neighborhood collecting poisonous and medicinal plants that I researched and identified, making my own 'potions' like a little shaman-scientist. My childhood dream was to be a doctor and surgeon, and would rush to the television every time there was a medical scene in a movie or TV show.

Another deep and highly specific interest when I was young was Christian Theology and Apologetics. I think this predilection to philosophising has evolved into its current form in my research into mysticism and esoteric sacred traditions from different cultures around the world, as well as my interest in the intersections between spirituality and science.

However, I did not get the exposure to many spiritualities and cultures when I was a child. I was raised a God-fearing 'good Christian boy' under a very traditional Presbyterian Singaporean Chinese family that rejected all other spiritualities as superstition or the 'Devil's work'. I was insanely proficient in Protestant theology and would even debate in good faith with pastors on doctrinal topics such as Transubstantiation, Predestination, Creationism and more when I was as young as 8. I gave a short sermon in a small family international church in China when I was 11, and with my gifts in Theology my family thought that I wanted to be a pastor when I grew up if I did not choose to become a doctor.

This religious zeal, amplified by my ignorance of social norms and others' perceptions, and my penchant to go super deep into things, meant that I had a radical fundamentalist phase in my late childhood. I remember going on an online gaming forum (which I was part of the modding and coding community) when I was in my early teens, and attempted to convert people to Christianity by creating a thread with a post in the style of a 'fire and brimstone' sermon. From the innocent but misguided perspective of my young self then, I simply wanted to share and sincerely thought that I was helping others with my knowledge. Regardless, my pleas for them to 'repent and be saved' weren't taken very well and caused quite a stir in that webspace.

Selective Mutism

Despite my intense passion for sharing my knowledge and interests, I still was seen as a quiet child by many. I either spoke a lot and very eloquently, or not at all. I also only spoke to some people, and not much at all to others. This was true especially in my Kindergarten and early Primary years, and I slowly grew out of it as I aged.

Simple social interactions and small talk were difficult for me. I only spoke a lot when the person or topic interested me. Physical touch and verbal expressions were precious and intense to me and I would only be open to giving and receiving if I were very close and comfortable with the person.
I didn't understand why I had to greet people such as elders when I met them. It wasn't that I was actively averse to the idea of greeting them, but most of the time I wasn't even aware of the situation in which I was expected to do so. I remember during family gatherings such as Chinese New Year, my older relatives such as my aunts and grandparents would misunderstand that I was being rude and disrespectful.

ADHD

My deep but diverse and varied interests may be influenced by the fact that my diagnosis of ASD came with the comorbidity of ADHD. I was very restless and could not focus well as a child. I had to change around 5 kindergartens, as when there was a window in the classroom, I would get distracted and look outside and daydream.

Constantly being distracted was caused by a lack of general executive functions and emotional regulation, but also an insatiable curiosity for life and the things around me. My mind was constantly moving at breakneck speed and thinking about multiple perspectives. And with the emotional regulation of a child, furthermore stunted (or enhanced) by my neurodiversity, this was a combination that led to uncontrollable energy, hyperactivity. I was either very understimulated, or hyperstimulated. I could not focus on daily tasks, but was hyper-focused in areas that intrigued me. I was super absent-minded for everyday matters, but had super capacity for memory and detail for things that I was deeply interested in.

Hypersensitivity

The restlessness I had as a child was not just due to my ADHD, but was also caused by a hypersensitivity to sensorial input due to ASD.

There is a common stereotype that autistic people have no emotion/feelings and that we are 'insensitive'. (Autistic people do have feelings, and they care about your feelings too!) However, it is exactly the opposite, as we can be over sensitive to certain things and phenomena. This manifested in some interesting abilities such as perfect pitch which I only discovered later in my life.

I was sensitive to both sensorial qualities and formal/affective qualities. I was selectively touch-phobic and super saliva-phobic. In terms of clothing, texture is very important. I was super sensitive to pokey or scratchy textures and could only wear certain clothes.

On a formal level, I had specific preference even to certain features of clothing such as collars and buttons. Certain symbols, forms and patterns affect me in powerful but interesting/unexpected ways. I had a phase around Primary 1 and 2 when I refused to wear buttoned shirts/school uniform outdoors unless within the paradigm of the school compound, at home, or in the school bus/car.

I am not sure whether this dislike for buttoned shirts came from an aversion to the form itself, or also the contexts, paradigms, and experiences that the forms are associated with. But looking back, I think it was a combination of both, as there was definitely an emotional component to the affective implications in wearing a school uniform (and in extension, buttoned shirts) and its associations with the institutional. This aversion to buttoned shirts still stays with me to this day in the form of my disdain for polo tees. To this day, I refuse to wear polo tees (unless I really have too, such as for work).

Dis-ease and Allergies

My hypersensitivity to sensory input was reflected psychosomatically with the physio-biological state of my body. I was riddled with allergies and was hospitalised multiple times for asthma. I also had chronic rhinitis that did not allow me to breathe through my nose, and had to breathe through my mouth all the way until I was in my twenties. My tonsils were perpetually swollen and caused serious infections, and I had to go through surgery when I was around 7 to take them out. I saw the photos of the tonsils after surgery, they were the size of ping pong balls.

It was the chronic discomfort and general dis-ease in daily life that also impaired my ability to focus and be fully present in my body and function optimally in social situations. I could not breath properly and felt sickly most of the time. Therefore, I was always in my head, disconnected with my sensations of the body and the sensorial-kinesthetic aspect of the outer world. Ironically, my hypersensitivity therefore made me become more insensitive from the embodied and physical aspects of the world and created a certain dullness and unresponsitivity in my constitution.

This led to two other very definitive symptoms as an autistic child: clumsiness and stimming.

Clumsiness

You would think that with more sensorial sensitivity and input, I would be hyper aware and responsive to situations. But it was usually too much for my brain to process and even passing a ball towards me would blank me out and cause me to fumble.

I had significant developmental delays in my gross psychomotor skills and kinesthetic awareness. I was super bad at sports, especially team ones where it requires both social and physical coordination, and this led me to be quite isolated from my peers when I was young all the way up to my teenage years. Conversely, I was great in fine motor-skills and was particularly good at solitary detailed work with my hands such as drawing, painting and sculpting.

Stimming

The hypersensitivity to external sensory input combined with the chronic internal dis-ease brought out certain coping mechanisms. Sometimes I will feel so uncomfortable, and to not be so overwhelmed, I zone out, or block it out, as I did not know how to process or react to it.

Another unconscious strategy I developed was to overstimulate myself with other things to distract myself from the sources of discomfort. This manifested in repetitive behaviours such as spinning, rocking, shaking parts of my body and making vocalisations. In Primary school, I would scare my classmates mid-lesson as I was imagining an entire movie on dinosaurs in my head, making random roaring noises and explosion sound effects in the middle of lesson while gesturing with my hands, fingers and body.

Another stimming habit I had in Kindergarten was spinning around at breakneck speed then suddenly stopping abruptly, seeing the world tilt or warp in my field of vision. It was so fun. When my mother asked me why I liked to spin, my kindergarten self told her, "I wanted to see the world from many angles."

While this was true, in hindsight, I realised it was also like inducing a kind of altered state of consciousness via the spinning - a mind-warping escape from reality.

Hyper-Systemisation and Routine

Besides strategies like shutting myself off into my own inner world and blocking out external (sensorial) input, the familiarity of routine was something that allowed the comfort and a sense of certainty and control from the confusing and disorienting world around me. I would like to eat only certain foods, wear certain clothes and listen to certain kinds of music.

My music taste was very different from others since I was young. In Primary school, it used to be all Christian worship music, Opera and Classical music. Even today, my playlist is still highly organised, with a highly specific internal order. For example, during my recent phase exploring Hinduism, I had a series of mantra playlists organised by days of the week based on astrological associations of the Deities:
Sunday: Sun - Surya Mantras (with other Sun associated deities such as Rama and Matangi)

Monday: Moon - Shiva Mantras (as Shiva wears the crescent on his head, and also Bhuvaneshwari)

Tuesday: Mars - Murugan and Hanuman Mantras (and also Bagalamukhi)
Wednesday: Mercury - Ganesha (with other Mercury/Vishuddhi associated deities such as Krishna and Lalita Tripura Sundari)
Thursday: Jupiter - Guru and Vishnu Mantras (and also Tara)
Friday: Venus - Devi Mantras (and all Mahavidyas, but particularly Kamala)
Saturday: Saturn - Kali and Hanuman Mantras (as Shani protects Hanuman bhaktas)

I would just listen to these playlists on repeat as I go about my day. This ended up in the unexpected ability to chant many long extended mantras by heart such as the Lalita Sahasranama, Devi Kavacham, and the Kanda Sashti Kavasam.

Relating to systems based on astrological correspondences, nowadays a model that I still keep as an adult is how I choose what to wear to work. For every day of the week, there is a colour for my shirt I wear to work based on elemental and planetary correspondences. This system allows me to be time and mentally efficient as I don't have to think so much about what to wear each day. Just follow the system - and I will look good and also have a reasonably varied presentation to others throughout the week. A big part is to build redundancy within the system itself (such as having multiple shirts in different styles for each colour, or having secondary colours for each day which I could choose from), so it allows for flexibility and choice.

Over the years, however, I have learnt to stray from comfort of familiarity occasionally, as well as respond to contingent events. It was also this ability to hyper-systemise that ironically allowed me to improve on my social skills later in life, by evaluating and reshaping my mental models of reality and social dynamics.

Refuge in a Different Land

So this was where I started out from, the bedrock of my journey that was to come. Despite having all these difficulties and differences, I remained a happy child. Most of the part I was oblivious to the extent of how I was different from others and how others saw me. I was sickly, but I had a brief period of refuge and respite when I went to China in my late Primary school years. It also marked the first turning point of my journey of healing, and also watered the seed of awareness of Self and Other.

My body healed and started to grow strong on a physical level. Despite the harsh cold winters in Northern China, my allergies were greatly reduced, to the point where my asthma totally went away. The low environmental humidity, cool temperate climate, and access to excellent Traditional Chinese Medicine did good to my body.

I did not attend an international school but went to a local Primary school instead. Being the only Singaporean amongst local Chinese students, my fellow classmates and schoolmates treated me as a foreign student. Being from a more 'developed country' also meant that many even looked up to me. Even though I was different, they did not think that I was weird - I was supposed to be different (from them) anyway.

I studied the same material and did the same tests as everyone, but most of the time I was also doing my own stuff during class, such as drawing my own comics and encyclopedias. I even had the time to read the GCE O-Level science textbooks and even the Christian Bible back-to-back a few times. My classmates probably thought it was unusual, but they were not averse to it. My weird or unusual (verbal) communication patterns were also masked to certain extent by expected differences in competencies of language between me and my Chinese schoolmates. Most of my passionate sharing was received as either unusual or refreshing, and I was even invited to teach the class English during English lessons by the teachers. My talents, interests and uniqueness were respected and celebrated rather than shunned. This unique social setting in a foreign land gave me space to explore, be myself and be accepted by others.

Little did I know, it was only after this when I went back to my very own people, that my difference with others became starkly known. The pain that was to come was the start of a rude awakening to reality. Oh, how ignorance is bliss!

The Prodigal Child
In Search of a 'Better Self'

I returned from China when I was in Lower Secondary, joining a neighborhood school mid-term. It was then that I really struggled to fit in and bond with my Singaporean peers.

When I was in a foreign land, my difference was expected and even celebrated at times. When one is in one's own culture, being 'too different' is punished - people expect you to behave in certain ways and assume that you know how to.

I was seen as weird for my lack of awareness and incompetence in social situations. I would forget simple social customs and gestures such as saying thank you, or giving gifts during occasions. I would neglect to inform my class and groupmates about things when it would affect them. I would cut people off when they are speaking, not being aware of the cues of when to come in, or whether the other person has finished their point. All these behaviours caused my peers to see me as rude, selfish or self-absorbed.

I did try to fit in though, a developed sort of a 'nice guy' personality. I tried less to stick out and tried to figure out what my peers were interested in or thought was 'cool', even changing my playlists to learn about the teenage trends of the time. I was a people pleaser and was quite weak and weird in my personality, leading to me becoming an easy target for bullies.

I tried but struggled to form connections with others. In an effort to connect, I would make jokes that are not relevant to the situation or to the people I was talking to. I remember making puns on red blood cells when my classmates didn't know what the word 'erythrocyte' meant. I was met with puzzled stares and seen as a smartypants and a show-off.

I would be very curious and overly-enthusiastic in classes (especially Biology and all of the Sciences and Humanities) and alway ask and answer questions. My class would collectively groan when it was time for recess and I would naively raise my hand to ask one last question at the end of the lesson, keeping the entire class back.

Not fitting in with my peers and being unable to relate to them, I ended having more fulfilling relationships with my teachers and elders. I remember even challenging the teacher in class on the final 1 mark on my biology paper, as I was marked wrong for an answer I gave that was outside of the syllabus. I ended up getting the mark and scoring full marks for that exam.

The teachers loved it. I was an 'excellent student' that validated their teaching. However, I was not a typical 'goody-two-shoes' that only obeyed rules and studied only whatever material they presented, but one with a rebellious but intellectual streak that would be willing to challenge them. My classmates did not see it that way through, and were less appreciative of my enthusiasm, and I became known in school as the 'teachers' pet'. Unbeknownst to me, schoolmates were even making bets during O-levels on who would get the top-scorer in our school, either me, or this other unassuming student-leader whose academic throne I usurped since joining the school.

I was also bullied for my looks and horrible sense of fashion. In Lower Secondary, students were supposed to wear short pants (the seniors wore long pants). My peers were altering their uniforms, wearing their pants/shorts low and baggy (the teenage fashion trend then) at the hips with cool belts, and styling their hair in 'illegal' ways. Being totally oblivious to fashion norms I would come to school with my shorts worn very high like a nerd, and I quickly became the laughing stock of not just my class but the entire cohort.

Me and my brother (who is also on the spectrum) have very small eyes, and were always teased for it even since Primary school. There was once in secondary school, a student of another race from a neighboring class yelled across the school hall one morning during assembly, "Go back to China you weird Cheena nerd (or 'CheeNerd')!" while making 'small/slanted eyes' at me. This complex of 'not looking good' enough has haunted me for years after that, and even till this day, sometimes I catch myself thinking the very same thoughts that I look weird or I was born ugly.

Bullying got so bad that it extended to the virtual sphere. It was the early days of the internet, with the rise of blogging culture. In the spirit of over-sharing and being socially unaware, I treated my blog like a journal and wrote very personal stuff including my thoughts on other schoolmates and how I felt lonely.

Being ignorant of the possibilities and the risks of cyberspace, the worst happened when I confided in my blog about my feelings for my secondary school crush and her then-boyfriend. I started receiving death threats in my chat box on my blog by the boyfriend's supporters, and soon, I was shunned and gossiped about around my entire school.

Here is an extract of a piece of writing from my Secondary School blog:

"Love your friends, for it is they who keep you from falling. Love your enemies, for they are the ones who build you up.

Blessed is the one who has friends. Blessed is the one who has adversaries. Pity for the one who has none.

For it is his deeds that go unheeded, his words that go unspoken, his feelings that go unannounced. He is the wanderer of the earth. When he talks, silence replies. When he ponders, his thoughts melt away in time. Silence is the worst reprimand and loneliness breeds suicide.

He lives in a world so full of people. Crowds, overpopulation. Yet he lives like a hermit. Starvation amidst plenty. As though one was the only person in the world. To him: A bustling crowd - a deserted jungle. The multitude - the sands of a desolate desert.

This wanderer, he reaches out his hand. "Help me!" He pleads. The leaves rustle, the sands rattle. Nothing happens.

Finally the wanderer dies, marooned upon this land he never called 'home'."

All these culminated into a crippling knot of worthlessness and shame within me. This feeling of loneliness and knowledge that I was different was the seed of my journey of self transformation in my late teenage years.

The Loss of Innocence

When I was young, innocent, and in my own world, I thought that everyone was my friend. Initially, I carried many ideals, dreams and fantasies of the world - a naive belief of a romanticised version of the world that is not necessarily grounded in reality and awareness of others. However, it did provide me with joy and some form of meaning as a refuge.

It was only after I got bullied badly and left without many friends, that I was forced to face the harsh cruelty of reality and humanity. I realised that not everyone was, and could be my friend. People did not match up to these ideals (as I too, had idealised them) and I could not trust them and myself anymore.

Realising that the world is not like what I imagined or thought it was, my trust in the world was also destroyed and it caused me to become bitter and resentful. But in a way, it was also not just a bitterness towards the world, but ultimately a resentment towards myself and my upbringing. It was a loss of my innocence.

There was a point where the pain of trying to be myself became too much. I told myself 'enough'. I wanted to become accepted and loved by people around me - no matter the cost. I wanted to 'fit in', because I was the weird one, and I was the problem. I wanted to be one of the 'cool crowd', because if I was, I would never be lonely again. I set out to actively learn social skills, desiring to 'change myself for the better'.

But was it 'for the better'? Waking up from 'my own world' and dismantling the childhood reverie also meant that I simultaneously reevaluated and rejected a lot of the perspectives and worldviews I grew up with, including matters of belonging, faith, religion and spirituality. I threw away a lot of the values I held dear since childhood to explore new ones. I swung to the other extreme. This was a transformation from the religious good boy to a party animal that relied on alcohol and cigarettes to get by socially.

'Leaving Home'

To be a 'prodigal child', one would have to leave their family home and their inherited values for 'greener pastures'. Hence, I would need to backtrack a bit to talk about my family history and parental influences.

As the oldest child, I had a lot of expectations and responsibilities put onto me. Growing up in a traditional and conservative Christian family with overbearing parents meant I had little chance to develop my own sense of self, and assert my own preferences and wants. It was from this restrictive environment that I had to rebel and start finding myself in my self-development journey. I was the 'Golden Child' of the family, but ended up becoming the 'Black Sheep'.

Got my scientific side from my dad, and the artistic sensibilities from my mom. My dad was a high achiever, a President Scholar and an Aerospace engineer. If there was a genetic basis for ASD, I probably inherited it from his lineage. He was brilliantly intelligent, but not very good at relating to people and expressing his emotions.

My mother was the exact opposite. She was a social butterfly with magnetism and presence. An SBC actress in her younger days, she was at the peak of her famous break when she quit her career in television to go into education due to having me and my brother. Her good looks, social mores, and charming but dominant personality meant that her presence was also a huge influence in my life, and at the same time, I was also always in the shadow of her brilliance.

I would have to give my parents credit in my journey of transformation. I inherited my mother's thirst for the spotlight and need for human connection. I also inherited my dad's over-analytical intellect that came with crippling perfectionism and anxiety, but allowed me to reflect, learn and apply myself effectively. The high expectations from my parents gave me a drive to excel in life, but also a self-esteem dependent on the approval of others. I carried along with me this attitude even when I rejected my previous upbringing and personality.

Therefore, faced with the prospect of self-discovery, I had an over-inflated and grandiose image of self that I could achieve whatever I wanted to achieve and, and at the same time, a crippling sense of inadequacy and dissatisfaction with my self-image and current situation. This hunger, even though unconsciously misguided or pathological at that time, was the ignition that actually allowed me to take positive action in the first place. The dissatisfaction of the current state of my life, and the obsessive need to be liked and to be accepted created the drive and the belief (no matter how unrealistic) that I could change myself and my circumstances.

So this was how I started my journey, with shame and self-loathing. I held the belief that I was 'not normal' - Something was 'wrong with me' and I needed to work on myself to be liked and accepted. Even though I had a 'growth mindset', it was coming from a place of lack - that I was not (good) enough.

I was running away from my past. I hid the ugly and undesirable sides of myself because of shame. Shedding away my past self, I did not know who I am and what I could be. But I (thought I) knew what I was and what I did not want to be.

The First Step

I started small, on personal behaviours which I could exert a certain amount of awareness and control. It was a highly logical and analytical approach of fixing myself, 'using my mind to solve my mind' and regulating my behaviour.

For example, one of the first behaviours I worked on was eye contact. In technical application, I took baby steps. Instead of looking at people's eyes from the get-go, I started by looking at people's 'third eye' area as it was less intense than looking directly into their eyes, slowly conditioning myself to the discomfort and upping the intensity as I went along.

Internally, this is a summary of the process:

I identify the feeling that led to the aversion of the desired behaviour (in this case, eye contact).

I feel fear and anxiety.

I then determine the source/reason for the fear through reflection and analysis, and what underlying beliefs I had that gave rise to these fears.

Was it because I was afraid of getting rejected? Or was it because I was afraid that it would actually go well and I would be stuck in a conversation that I could not handle or leave? Was it due to sensory overload, and if so, what ways can I minimise and manage the overload, or build mental and emotional capacity to handle greater intensities?

I then evaluate whether the reasons and beliefs around the fear are sound and relevant to the context. What are the worse case scenarios that would happen? Are they really founded in actual reality in the current context? Is my fear of looking at someone in their eyes rational - do people really not like me when I look at them? Or do they actually expect and wish me to do so in social situations?

Decide to apply the behaviour and gain reference experiences. After evaluating, if I found that the reasons for the fear were not relevant, or if the rewards of the desired behaviour far outweigh the risks, I would try to enact the behaviour in different settings. This allowed me to gain reference experiences of execution of the behaviour and insights to people's perception of that said behaviour. As I applied more eye contact in daily life, did not receive rejection and had more and more positive responses, I not only gained confidence and competency through practice, but it also made the initial fears less and less relevant.

This was a mental model and process that I would use throughout my late teenage years and young adulthood to modify and refine my behaviours and beliefs. First, I worked on the most immediate autistic tendencies that came in the way most in my relationships with others. I worked on my saliva and touch phobia, building tolerance to handshakes, hugs, kisses and sharing food, and normalising such desirable behaviours in my life so that I could fit in and connect with people better. I also worked on managing and suppressing certain proclivities such as my ticks and weird body language so that I could present a 'good impression'. It was only later in life when I went to some therapy in my university years for a depressive episode, that I realised I was unknowingly doing something akin to 'Cognitive Behavioural Therapy' since young on myself.

I slowly build up tolerance in social situations. First, it was learning to be ok with being uncomfortable. Then, learning to be functionally aware within the discomfort. After I could handle basic human interactions and simple conversations, I could start focusing more on developing my social awareness. Being more comfortable looking people in the eyes and watching their facial expressions meant that I was able to pick up more and more cues. Being more comfortable with a conversation also meant that I could be mentally free to pay attention to the situation and reactions of the people around me.

So I continued to work this way, dealing with aspects of my personality, behaviours and awareness one by one. Armed with books and the gift of the internet, I poured my heart and mind into the study of psychology and social dynamics, wanting to understand how the mind works and what makes people tick. I was constantly modifying my behaviours and trying out new things by analysing and critiquing my thoughts, words and actions.

An Organised Practice

At first, the way I went about it was quite haphazard and chaotic. During National Service, with access to my new found purchasing power and freedom from my family, I relied on alcohol and cigarettes as "social lubricants" for learning. I basically tried, crashed and burnt (by facing rejections after rejections) and got up again - Learn and apply, rinse and repeat, until I 'figured things out'. I would drink, go out and do approaches in low stakes situations such as bars and nightclubs and try to make friends with people.

Even then, there was some method to the madness. These 'field work' was a means for me to get those reference experiences and to put my research into practice. Gradually, I developed a targeted and progressive practice, focusing on one aspect at a time mainly. Sometimes during nights out I would focus on eye contact and vocal tonality. Sometimes I would focus on body language and physical boundaries. Sometimes I would focus on humour and conversation skills, sometimes on being more assertive. At the end of the night, I will go home and list out the things that went well and did not go so well, and analysed them, and then repeat the process.It was a lot of 'sucking it up' and being desensitised to rejection. I had to be ok and be able to hold my emotional state in difficult or challenging situations such as people not giving me good responses, giving me weird looks and finding me suspicious.

Then on a reflective level, it was understanding my triggers and not allowing the external environment and opinions of people affect me so much, not taking things personally and perservering even when I did not feel like it.

Soon I got decently good that I even started getting free drinks in clubs, other favours and special access from the people I made friends with. I was even able to apply the understanding and skills I learnt in such situations into 'sober everyday life'.

The Competent Masker
The Charming Shapeshifter

Soon after I got most of the social basics down and could pass off as a 'normal' well-adjusted person, I read up and practiced in multiple intersectional domains of relating to people: (this is a non-exhaustive list)

Sales and Persuasion
Negotiation and Mediation
Teaching and Coaching
Leadership and People Management
Public Speaking
Storytelling
Acting and Performer's Training

I deliberately placed myself in high pressure social situations such as making sales pitches to strangers. I figured that if I got this down pat, I would also be able to transfer the skills to daily social situations - as we are, always in a way, 'selling' ourselves, or at least, communicating an image/impression of ourselves to others.

In such social situations where there is an agenda and the pressure to make something happen, there was an even more quantifiable metric for success and failure in which I could measure my progress, which was important for me in this stage of learning.

Stopping strangers on the street and getting them to trust you and buy something, requires me to get their initial interest, and to hold their attention long enough to get to the meat of my pitch, and then get their compliance to close the deal.

There were so many things to learn and apply. I learnt how to make people feel comfortable in my presence and to build rapport and trust. I explored how people perceive value and how I could convey value in a way that did not seem try-hard or desperate. I explored how to persuade people by making people interested in me or what I was saying, by establishing emotional relevance and spiking their emotions through provocative expressions or through humour.

I also learnt to calibrate, finding the balance between what is surprising and unusual (which can generate interest) and what is familiar and comfortable (which builds trust). Other forms of calibration include balancing assertiveness and receptivity, speaking and listening, finding the limits of how I can assert my energy and express my personality/message in different situations. I also worked on reading and listening to people, figuring out what their comfort levels, what their values and interests are, and adjusting my approach in different contexts accordingly.

This was also a stage of my social development where I discovered the magic of subcommunication. I gained awareness of non-verbal cues such as body language and micro-expressions. I also learnt that many times it's not what I say, but how I say something - how to play around vocal tonality, inflexion and pacing to achieve desired effect and affect.

In a more inner sense, I learnt the value of congruence in engendering trust and confidence, believing in what I say and in my product (or whatever I represented), and a congruence between my thoughts, words and actions. I also learnt that I can affect my emotional state with my physical state, and vice versa (which opened up the door to developing mind-body connection later).

Mental Models and Frameworks

The technical approach was a pretty forceful approach to 'fixing my personality'. In the earlier stage of my development, learning in social situations was pretty artificial or manufactured. At first, I relied on many routines which I crafted meticulously, and built up a vocabulary of different responses for different situations.

When applying new concepts or adopting new behaviours and attitudes, I had to 'force the behaviour', and test it out in the field. Some things don't work and do work, and I have to go back to the drawing board, reflect, recalibrate and test out my hypotheses. After a while discovering what works and what was most suitable for my personality and values, I developed a certain level of competence and awareness. This further reduced my mental and cognitive load, that I could be even more present and pay attention to the actual social interactions themselves, and get to try out even more things. However, within my head, I was constantly calculating, analysing and assessing the social situation, the state of the interactions, and signs people are giving me.

I built various mental frameworks which I constantly update and reevaluate, understood group theory, and was able to start applying myself across a wide range of social paradigms. This required me to develop awareness of the nuances between different social contexts, which came from a large data set and sample size of meeting and interacting with so many people in different kinds of situations. This ability allowed me to connect with people from diverse backgrounds, groups and cultures.

Cultivating Openness

Even though one aspect of Autism is being very risk-averse (think selective mutism, eye contact, touch and saliva phobia) and being attached to one's routines and structures, my encounter with loneliness and shame in my teenage years led me to overcompensate by having a lot of friends. I developed sort of a complex where I prided myself in being able to mix with many different kinds of people. I took this as a challenge and trained myself to talk to everyone, and learnt from all kinds of people from all walks of life (even some questionable ones). It was a less naive evolution of the 'everyone is my friend' attitude I had since I was a child. I found that there was always something to be learnt from anyone, and also if not, the interaction itself.

In hindsight, this openness and 'lack of judgment' also stemmed from an initial weakness in personality, and thus I was able to use it to off-set the phobic, risk-averse aspects of my autistic personality. I probably rated quite high on 'Openness' on the Big 5 Personality Trait assessment as I was very accepting of people and experiences. I loved to share since I was young and had a weak-theory-of mind which resulted in a lack of solid sense of self and boundaries. The ability to empathise was my greatest weakness when I was younger, and I was taken advantage of many times in my Primary school days. In my teenage and young adult years, I was also easily influenced and led me into some questionable relationships and destructive lifestyle choices.

This very weakness also turned out to be one of my greatest strengths later in life. As I matured and had a better sense of myself and my values, this sense of curiosity and non-judgement allowed me to connect with and learn from many people.

I think throughout my journey, I was blessed to still have a presence of criticality in the background and that allowed me to learn and pick up behaviours, attitudes, perspectives and frameworks (that I liked or found useful) from a diverse sample size of people and experiences through a reflective and analytical process. It was good to be critical and discriminating, but it was also good to be open and non-judgemental.

The shift from the mindset of being critical about the success/failure of every single interaction and bashing my self-worth all the time, into a mindset of being curious, non-judgemental and wanting to learn, marked a significant development in my competency and ease in social situations.

Degree of Self-Identification

Settings like cold-sales were good training wheels, due to the high volume of social interactions and the relative task-oriented nature of these interactions. These tasks, being in a relatively 'artificial' and simulated setting, buffers the pain of rejection by allowing plausible deniability of the identification with my 'self-concept'. I could shift our focus to evaluating the ability to achieve a certain role, rather than my fundamental, intrinsic worth as a person. It was relatively anonymous, and there was disassociation and distance from the perception(s) of my actions and behaviours with my identity and value as a person. "I was just doing my job." - I was not selling myself, but selling a product. I was not representing myself, but representing a company or organisation.

Conversely, I discovered the level of pain in rejection is proportionate to the interaction's degree of identification with the persona. The most painful rejections are the ones you go out representing 'yourself'. This covers situations such as going into clubs, parties, public speaking and networking events, and any situation where I engage people and try to connect as 'myself'.

However, even then, high pressure situations like nightclubs were still a playground for my practice as they provide a relative degree of anonymity and a high volume of people to work with. There are so many people, with loud music, darkness and flashing lights. People are mostly drunk, and most people wouldn't remember you after that night (unless you made such an impression or high quality of connection.) This allowed me to be less attached to how people would perceive me, and allowed me to really explore and express the different dimensions of my personality.

Letting Go of Outcome

In contrast to task-oriented social situations such as sales, where the parameters and intent of the interactions are clearly defined, daily social interactions are a bit different. People don't like to feel you have an agenda or that you 'need something from them' when making friends. A shift of perspective was required, which is to be more process-oriented than outcome-oriented.

A technique I would use for making friends with strangers is to do something very out of the ordinary; out of what my 'usual self' would do. One such example was an exercise I used to do - going up to strangers on the street and trying to start a conversation by opening with, "Would you like a cup of tea?" in an exaggerated Queen's English accent.

On one hand, this behaviour is so absurd that it allows suspension of disbelief in others. Executed with attention and basic respect paid to the boundaries such as personal space, people just automatically accepted it as it is so beyond the conventions of everyday reality, and could find the humour or intrigue behind it. It was like the analogy of 'it's so bad it's good."
But on a deeper level, people also accepted it as I first accepted it first. The absurdity of my behaviour is so out of my 'normal' conception of self (and one's default behaviour and personality) and hence paradoxically allows me to let go of the outcome and 'be normal' (and actually find humour) in the situation. I saw it as 'something normal' and carried myself well and with confidence. I did not come across as nervous or creepy, worrying whether the interaction will fail or not. It's so bad that you expect it to fail anyway. And then it works.

This discovery of non-attachment to outcome was my first initiation and glimpse into the magic of flow in my relationships.

The Magic of Flow

Although I remained technical and analytical in my approach towards self-development and relationships, there are instances where I have allowed myself to be taken over by 'the flow'.

Psychologist Mihaly Csikszentmihalyi describes being 'in the flow' as an optimal cognitive state in which one is completely engrossed in an activity, where the conditions of challenge and competency are balanced optimally.

To get into flow in social interactions, I would first have to learn to manage my emotional state and energy levels. On an inner level, this was first done by slowly working on my beliefs, attitudes and perspectives about myself in social settings. This allowed me to focus on carrying myself more confidently and cultivate the view people are going to like me and receive me positively.

At an outer level, I worked on assuming interest and rapport, and interacting with people positively and confidently even though I may not feel like it at the moment or believe myself yet to be an attractive or interesting person. At first it was a lot of 'faking till I made it', as I got better and got more experiences with positive interactions with people, it got easier and easier.

Having developed a certain level of confidence and competency, it was then shifting the focus to less being self-conscious or task-conscious, and to enjoying the interaction itself. Shifting from conscious competence to unconscious competence took off a lot of the cognitive and emotional load in my interactions and allowed me to focus on the interaction itself. It is good to have standards, goals and expectations, but in an actual social interaction I have to let it take the backseat and let go of my expectations of how people are going to perceive me and how well the interaction is going. This allowed me to shift to a more process-oriented way of being.

Afterwhich, it was a matter of balancing between being process and task-oriented. Sometimes being task-oriented is required, such as going for the close in sales, or getting someone's contact in a networking event. I still have to move the interaction forwards and be sincere and assertive in my needs and wants. I am still playing a role and performing a version of myself, but I am in the social interaction itself, I try to be in the moment and pay attention to the other person.

Being prepared helps. For example, if I am prepared before a lesson or a presentation, during the actual event I can be in flow and really focus on connecting with the audience, rather than being worried about or tripped up by technical issues. This was also what my rehearsed stories and personally crafted social routines were good for in social situations. I relied on them to set the comfort of the setting, get the momentum of the conversation going, so that it gets past the 'activation energy' for flow to happen.

There are times where I set up the conditions and do everything right, then suddenly I'm in flow and the social interaction takes on a life of its own. Friendships and connections unfold as a natural process and meaningful relationships are forged.

These are the positive experiences that I remember dearly and integrate into my being.

Just having fun and playing actually gave me the best lessons. My best connections with people came when I was being free in my interactions, and not to be stuck in my own head when I am with them. There is a right time and place for everything. I would leave the serious analysing and reflection when I got home and spend my alone time.

Discovering flow was where I also started relying less on crutches such as alcohol to be able to have fun and positive social experiences. It was also what allowed me to flow organically between different situations and groups of people.

Becoming Skillful

Slowly but surely, I mastered the ability to skillfully switch between and present different sides of myself depending on the social contexts at hand. It was like social code-switching and it almost became 'second nature'.
I was so good at it that after a while, most people could not tell that I was autistic. I was even perceived as more 'socially successful' than others. In university, starting from a clean slate (with again the 'social armour' of being in a foreign land), I became somewhat of a 'cool guy', even so much that many friends started coming to me for relationship advice.

And because I studied and worked on this aspect of my life so much and built it from ground zero, I realised that I could actually give pretty good advice. I could look at someone and their interactions, and break it down for them step-by-step, aspect-by-aspect, and share with them where and when they did not do so well, and where they had ignored or crossed (social and personal) boundaries. Through their sharing with me and the manner in which they articulate about themselves, their partners and the situation, I could also tell where they held certain limiting beliefs and unhealthy perspectives.

From what I observed, many people cruise through life getting by with 'just enough' social awareness. Born with 'good enough' social skills, they grow up without encountering a dire need to develop the competencies and a solid metacognitive framework in which to reflect and make sense of their behaviours and their relationships.

Hence, they lack the practice to manage their emotions and the emotions of others effectively and skillfully. As they don't really go out much or actively connect with people outside their social circles and comfort zone, they lack reference experiences and the ability to see from different points of view.

It is crazy to see that even as a person with 'high functioning' ASD, I could see clearly from my observations of others that there are so many supposedly 'neurotypical' people that are so bad with people and relationships.

Struggles of a 'High Functioning Autistic'

As my masking grew more proficient, it struck me that most people I met did not perceive me as an autistic person. In popular parlance, I became a 'high-functioning autistic' and I usually eschew revealing this aspect of myself to others until I have gotten to know them better. I found this to be an alienating experience - as much as I hope to be regarded as a neurotypical individual, I simultaneously wish that people would accept me for who I am wholeheartedly.

When my autistic and ADHD tendencies eventually and inevitably surfaced, I have had to invest a lot of emotional labour into salvaging these relationships. People were surprised by my behaviours and sometimes offended at my 'condition', and I have even had to convince them of its veracity. I vacillated between a deep-seated desire to be 'normal' and for my 'difference' to be treated with compassion and understanding. But my competencies at masking meant that I would be (unfairly) measured against the yardsticks of neurotypicality - until fractures begin to show on my mask(s).

The journey of the solitary hero with a thousand masks, is ultimately, still a lonely one.

The Dark Night of the Soul

The persona of the consummate masker shattered when I was grappling with a severe bout of depression at the tail end of my university life. I was battling a life-threatening health crisis, a difficult family situation, and this was compounded by the dissolution of an intimate relationship. The social anxieties and awkwardness that I tried so hard to fend off returned with a vengeance. It seemed like all my socio-emotional faculties were lost or broken. I was caught up in a vicious cycle of negativity and wound up being at a deeper end than where I was at when I was younger.

At least I was happy and blissfully ignorant when I was younger. What's worse than being ignorant and unaware, is being painfully aware of what 'I should' and 'should not do', but being unable to do it. This critical inner voice has done well so far being a tough teacher earlier in life in building up my persona, but now it was my greatest jailer and punisher. I was back to zero, or worse, sub-zero.

It felt so hopeless, that I thought I had 'fixed myself' and had "gotten over (my condition)". I thought I had 'cured' myself, I thought that I was no longer weird and would never be lonely again. But to see that everything I had built was so fragile that it could all crumble like that in a moment brought a sense of deep despair. As I had depended and identified with my mask(s) for so long, it had become an integral part of my sense of self, and losing it was intensely traumatic on top of the depression itself.

But that was exactly it. What I had built was a mask, or a 'meta-mask' - a persona that was built from a place of self loathing and self rejection, based upon what I felt others and the external world saw and thought of me. It was born because of pain, but I had not really faced the pain that was in me, but was running away from it. I did not see who I really was, but instead, denied it. I had good experiences, sure, but I had neglected myself. I was 'high on the world', but did not see how exhausted and weary I was inside.

I realised how alone I was all the time. By 'fixing myself', I had come to create a life and persona that was well received by others. But in the end, it was not really me that they accepted and loved, but a fabricated version of me that I chose to show them. Ironically, by chasing for love and acceptance, I ended up being more alienated towards myself and others.

The Belly of the Whale

Regardless of how unhealthy my relationship with myself was at the time, I was still blessed with patient and loving friends and family. Infact, I would say that they were one of the reasons I pulled through in the end.

They tried to help and hold space for me, and I frequently felt even more guilty and useless when I could not 'feel better' despite their efforts, and could not reciprocate their kindness and compassion. Utter hopelessness descended as I realised I did have loving relationships, but even in the presence of such connections, I could not feel happy and could not appreciate and receive their love. In this state of (self-)abandonment, it really felt to me that I would never ever experience love and happiness again. There must be something fundamentally broken about me and all the previous happiness in my life was a lie.

Living in the constant state of fear and despair poisoned my view of reality and caused me to act out in irrational ways. I was pushing people away, being very hurtful and uncompassionate to myself and others. However, deep inside, I also knew that this was an inner journey that only I could walk alone in the end.

Negative thoughts and feelings were my daily companions, looping endlessly. One thought generates a negative emotion, which then brings up another negative thought, which then triggers another negative emotion, which then brings up another negative thought, and another, and another, and another. It was like a snake eating its tail, spiraling downwards into the darkness.

After a while, I wasn't even feeling sad and anguished all the time. These unending and incessant thought loops were so much to the point where I became quite numb to everything. It was the state of being fully consumed with despair, as it was even too painful to have hope. Everything could be a trigger for overwhelming pain, so I closed myself off to reality. But being numb to the negative aspects of self, also meant that I was numb to all other aspects of being. Being disassociated with my pain meant also being deprived of the joys and pleasures in life.

Being depressed was like living within and acting out from the state of the 'Shadow' self perpetually. In the deafening silence of aloneness, fears and negative beliefs of self usually hidden within my unconscious were sublimated to the surface, and were never so clear. I was staring into the abyss and seeing the Beast lurking in the shadows.

Then, I looked at my life and my relationships so far, and realised the Beast was none other than me.

I was in the belly of the whale, surrounded with the demons of the self. It is a state of deep confusion and disorientation. All constructs of meaning and self were shaken to their core. The previous reality had disintegrated, and the previously solid sense of identity was slowly torn apart, piece by piece, by these ravenous demons that robbed me of my sense of vitality and certainty.

At the precipice of rationality and irrationality, of being and non-being, it was in this state of liminal existence, between the light and darkness of my consciousness, where the potentiality of new knowledge and becoming started to dawn.

The Taming of the Beast

When one is at rock bottom, there was no longer any way but to either perish and end it all, or to carry on living and start the slow climb upwards.

In that state of deep ocean of darkness, I started opening up to feeling again. Swimming with the fishes, I learnt to be with these difficult feelings, to accept them and to understand them. I had to hold space for them in my being and watch them arise and pass, rather than to ignore, reject and suppress them further into my unconscious, or conversely, get consumed by them and caught up in the endless spirals of negativity. The healing process kicked in gradually and that implied confronting my demons (i.e. my insecurities, inadequacies and fears) while opening a space for myself to do so.

I have had to let go of my fears and attachments to a specific conceptualisation of myself and others. Meanwhile, I had created beliefs, frameworks and narratives that helped me navigate the world around me. These colour my perceptions and interpretations of everything. But sometimes, these got in the way of myself actually engaging the world for what it is, and also got in the way of forming a genuine connection with myself and others. In the state of depression, these perceptions and interpretations did not serve and protect me as they did before but instead caused more pain and despair. I had to again slowly let go of all the conditioning, limiting beliefs and dependency on what I have learnt. It was letting go of the expectations I had on myself - letting go of my attachments to the 'what ifs', the would'ves', 'could'ves' and should'ves'. I had to let go of all the resentment, anger, and sense of failure that came with not having these expectations, but also needs, met.

Then, I allowed myself to grief. For every narrative, every concept of self and other that I let go and died to, I grieved. I accepted my grieving as a natural response to a painful loss. I grieved the loss of my innocence, my relationships, and my sense of self. Doing so allowed me to work through my brokenness and be empowered by confronting the hidden or masked parts of myself which I was immensely ashamed of and disgusted with. I had to see them for what they truly are, real, human needs within me yearning to be met and accepted. I learnt to embrace these 'unpalatable' and 'selfish' aspects of myself I have kept locked up in a cage, thereby overcoming my clinging to the many masks that were devised to 'protect' me (or my inner child) in the first place.

Embracing these shadow parts of myself entailed having to cope with the fear of non-acceptance and of not being loved. The strategies I have previously mobilised to "fix" myself (e.g. masking) have ceased to serve their purpose. I was therefore compelled to change the ways in which I relate to myself, including being loving and kind to my past and present selves. As I picked up and mended the shattered pieces of myself with self-love and compassion as the glue, I emerged with a fuller understanding of the many aspects of myself.

The path of healing is not one of fixing
Not of striving to attain something
Nor a work to reclaim something
But a process of recognising.

Just like the initial pain that woke my innocent child self up from the reverie of my childhood and started the journey of self-development (and denial), this deep inner pain during my depression was also a unmistakable signpost that revealed to me the areas in my life I was running away from and that needed care and presence.

It was an awakening to the aspects of myself hidden in plain sight, and appreciating the gifts that were already there within myself. It was looking at my brokenness and all the suffering I had been through, and recognising the beauty and wisdom that came with it. It was seeing all ignorance, stupidity and regrets in my life and recognising that even through it all, it was actually always me trying my best, because this little, innocent child inside only wanted to love and be loved.

I thought that it was a journey to reclaim my innocence. But then, I realised that my innocence was never lost in the first place.

Awakening to Presence

Slowly, the world started being beautiful again. I was being awakened to the beauty in others and myself. It was like one day I realised, "Oh, I am happy again." I never thought that I could be happy again, but then here we are.

As I healed from my depression, I gradually recovered my social skills too. I came to realise that what I had learnt was never lost, and that no experience was ever wasted or worthless. When I regained my social competencies, my relationship with them had also evolved.

This time it felt different, there was a deeper alignment of my heart, mind and actions. There was an opening of the heart - of love, acceptance and trust. Instead of using these social skills as a crutch for my personality, there is no more of all that over-analysing of what the person is going to say, what should be my response, what are their motivations, what is the context of the situation, etc. I became so much less dependent on that critical, analytical and theoretical 'nonsense', as that fundamentally came from a place of not trusting myself. I have come to know and trust that my tools, intellect, and my past experience will be there, and that I could respond to the situations accordingly. Coming from a place of trust, I could be fully present in my experience of the shared moment with the other person.

This alignment between my mind, heart and body also was a journey of learning. As you can remember from my poor psychomotor skills when I was young, I lived too much in my head, and had a disconnection to my body. Healing from my depression also radically changed my relationship with my body, and impelled me to pay attention and be present with it.

I started by getting back into sports and fitness, developing mind-muscle connection through calisthenics and other modalities. I then moved into practicing somatic practices such as Taichi, Qigong and Yoga, developing interoception and learning how to be with my body and my sensations - the full spectrum of experience of pain and pleasure, ease and tension (dis-ease). I also started performers' training, especially in physical theatre and contact improvisation, learning how to honour my impulses, such as desire, aversion and apathy, and to embrace the lines of flight and inspiration that emerge from them. My singing practice also allowed me to practice using my breath to connect my mind and body, connecting my physical and vocal expression with my (inner) voice and opening up to the entire expression of myself.

When looking to find one's 'truth, self and purpose', some people confuse 'looking within' with running away from the external world and the present immediate reality into their inner world of their own concepts, fantasies and ideologies. Then, we end up with more confusion and delusion, hiding behind illusory conceptualisations of what reality is, should be and could be, living only in the past or the future. What is truly alive is in the present. As I opened myself to the experience of life - its richness of sensations, its entire dimension of experience, the good and the bad, the uncertainty and flux, but also of infinite possibility, the world became alive in its constant state of being and becoming.

As I opened myself up to life, people also started naturally becoming more open to me and my presence.

To be present gives me presence. And to others, my presence is my greatest present.

Awakening to Authenticity
Embracing the Self

How can we uncover a more authentic sense of personhood? While authenticity may not be absolute, I have come home to a more authentic self by holding space for my thoughts, feelings and being with radical honesty as well as non-judgment. Besides being mindful of the background noise in my head, alongside the emotions in my body without being reactive to them, I have begun to honour (and assert) my needs and desires. I no longer attempt to escape from, repress or appraise myself based on what I think and feel.

One in which I seek to assert my needs/desires respectfully will be to delineate clear boundaries premised on my values, standards and expectations. The delineation of such boundaries presupposes that I am conscious of the value that I bring to the table as well as what I value in myself/others. Perhaps it is the law of attraction at play — I have observed that people have come to value me since I began accepting/valuing myself. And this time, what they valued was a version of me that is real and honest, and not a construct that I created to hide my flaws and insecurities. This also meant that relationships became even more effortless and fulfilling, as having values and knowing what I value also automatically filters the people who are disingenuous or incompatible in my life.

Awakening to a more authentic self requires inner work that exceeds the often cited cliche of "just be yourself" — a seemingly profound piece of advice that has little real-life utility. Most people, like me when I started out my journey, do not know ourselves. In addition, "being yourself" should ideally not be a smokescreen for a lack of self-awareness or for victim-posturing.

Awakening to Relationship Dancing with the Anima

When I became a public-school teacher, I was constantly overwhelmed with the intensity of having to teach multiple classes of forty students. These students demanded my undivided attention and now my scope of influence expanded to require me to be wholly present for these young minds. I was, after all, responsible for them. In other words, learning how to connect to my students (and other people) with intention and attention became an imperative.

In facilitating my students' learning, I had to nurture an atmosphere of trust and confidence to allow for these relationships and explorations to blossom. I saw how meaning and sense-making 'happened' organically between my students and I, as well as among themselves. I was infected by their zest for learning and life, and discovered the joy of holding space for my students, so that they could find themselves. Seeing them grow and transform, this period of my life was where I experienced so much beauty, innocence, love and meaning in my relationships. It was also where I discovered what it felt like to be truly accepted and respected, and loved.

According to Carl Jung's psychology, the Anima refers to a component of ourselves that is repressed, or embedded in our unconscious mind. Such repressed parts of ourselves may include the attributes of the opposite gender that one may identify with. These attributes, which are not usually accessible to the self, are then sought after, or projected onto the 'Other'. One's relationship with these qualities (within one's psyche and towards other people) also then massively colours the health and quality of all relationships with other people in one's life.

Being present to all of the 'Self' also means being fully open to the 'Other' - not just one's conceptualisations of the 'Other' projected onto others, but the 'Other' within the Self.

The search for the Self was also tied to the search for meaning, in others and within ourselves. As we carry around narratives that help us make sense of ourselves, of others, and of the world, I learnt to be more aware of my relationships with these narratives, holding space for non-judgement but also being mindful and clear.

Instead of clinging to my set expectations and narratives of the Self and Other, I started being fully open, fully giving and receptive to my own experience, and experience of others in a radical and vulnerable way. It was paying attention to affect and effect, and allowing whatever that is most alive and intimate to emerge. 'Meaning' then becomes something that is co-created by myself, others and the world. Relationships become like a dance, flowing between the Self and the Other. Dancing with others is not just a science, but an art, and art needs heart.

We all can probably recall an experience in our lives where we met someone and felt seen and heard so deeply that we could fully be ourselves, even much more than we could ever be towards ourselves alone. This is possible as only being fully present to oneself can we be fully present to others. And by being fully present with oneself and the other, we can also allow them to fully be themselves.

This was me finally opening up from 'my own world' to really developing theory-of-mind. Being in a relationship and forming a connection with someone is not done through, or done to figure myself out or figure someone else out - I can never figure myself and someone else out fully. But this process of mutual discovery is infinitely more exciting and beautiful, and the journey of discovery is always more fun with others around.

It dawned on me that my journey of finding myself, originally stemmed from a desire to connect with another. It was this self that wanted to be seen, heard, be accepted and loved. Conversely it was also true that to connect with the Other is inextricably bound up in the desire to connect with the Self.

Everything starts with emotion, and ends with an emotion.

My journey started with a search for (emotional) connection, and evolved along the way into a search for a 'self' that would be accepted by others. There was no point trying to be so caught up in the search for self, that I forgot what inspired my search in the first place - It was the search for meaning and connection. It was the search for love. Radical, unconditional love.

Conclusion
From Self to non-Self

I have been wearing masks and masking parts of myself for most of my life, to the point where my (ascribed and constructed) identities are merely a performance or a mode of impression management. Looking back on my journey, I started out with a weak sense of personhood, and also a sense of weak 'Other'-hood, or what psychologists would call 'a weak theory-of-mind'. However, I have learnt to transform these purported weaknesses into strengths. A large part of this transformation involved self-acceptance, and ironically through a dissolution of the (conditioned) self.

By the 'dissolution of the self', I mean a realisation of a particular attitude of 'non-self' that I need to cultivate - that of not clinging to egoistic constructs of the Self and Other. It is a slow but sure release of the dependencies to ways that I see myself, and see others, and the ways I see others see me. It was also letting go of this desperate seeking for this sense of self, whether in the people around me, or within my own head. I was finally coming to terms with my originally 'weak sense of self', not through rejection of the condition, and not through resigned acceptance, but a conscious, courageous embrace.

Because, what is this original 'Self' we are all supposed to 'have' anyway?

Paradoxically, when I shifted my experience of 'self' as a vibrant thing that is constantly being renewed, transformed and discovered every moment, constantly in flux and always impermanent, I could really start to cherish things, people, experiences and relationships in spite of the impermanence. In fact, it is the understanding and acceptance of impermanence that I can truly come to appreciate the preciousness and profoundness of the present moment. And paradoxically, when I shifted my focus from my preoccupation of self, is when I truly found myself. It was finally shifting my focus to finding the joy in my connection with others, that I started to find true fulfillment within myself.

Experiencing the multifaceted self-evolving and reflected through the richness of relationships around me, I came to realise that it was perfectly normal and natural to have many masks. We all have many 'selves' arising and emerging at different times and places, with different contexts and people. All these are part of me, but also not intrinsically me at the same time, and also a part of everybody all at once, and will continue to live on long after I am gone.

Having walked this journey so far, donning many masks and putting myself in many others' shoes, I realised that all of us (neurotypical or not) are not that different after all. We all carry masks for different situations and roles in our life; neurodivergent people just do the masking thing in a different level and manner. All of us all want to belong, to be seen, heard, appreciated and loved. It is not that masking is fundamentally 'bad', but when we forget ourselves and we hide our light under that mask, it does not do justice to us, and to the people who really deserve us.

Being different is hard, but not living to one's truth is harder.

Therefore, I shall end my story by sharing with you the most important thing that I have learnt in journey so far - the most profound but also most useless of all truths:

"Go, and just be yourself!"

Clement Wee's bio

He can be found at the Life Issues Transformed and Us Facebook group. Clement Wee is an experienced software developer who also has a keen artistic and
aesthetic side. Although he is unable to produce visual arts effectively due to non-verbal
learning disorder (NVLD), he nonetheless may produce visual arts. Since he was young, he has
been a talented (amateur) writer and recalls winning storytelling competitions at primary
school. He is particularly inspired by speculative fiction, especially those with elaborate
worldbuilding. He is a fan of Japanese culture, including manga, anime and onsen. He
also enjoys learning interesting historical facts about anywhere in the world.

In contributing to this anthology, Clement hopes to express a part of his life he hasn't

before, and let people understand this somewhat different experience. He is honoured

to be one of the writers/contributors for this work.

He has adopted "arixion" as his online and gaming handle since he was 10, as it is cool

Clement is one of the most knowledgeable people known to our and other circles. His grasp on all things Catholic is astounding. Clement is arguably the Most Valued Player in the Emmaus Catholic Toastmasters Club

Chapter Eleven

Limbo

By Clement Wee

Neither here nor there is a bad place to be, whether in fiction or in real-life. It is even worse when that is a descriptor for your state in life.

The other neurodivergents who contributed to this book can be placed somewhere on the concept of the Spectrum. If I think about it carefully, I would say that the Spectrum is a very abstract concept. Being off the Spectrum classifies you as a neurotypical; that's the current social definition. But if we were to classify the Spectrum as "the Wrong Planet" – and I know that there is an online community by that very name – then neurotypicals would be classified as "The Right Planet" or just "Earth", probably. But you know, there is a vast distance between Earth and Venus, the empirically closest planet; and that space contains rocks, and moons.

I guess I am in that space or am a moon. Unfortunately, this is the place where the analogy breaks. I am not sufficiently abnormal to be placed on the Spectrum, but just "off" enough not to fit with the "typical" crowd. Officially, my diagnosis is non-verbal learning disorder, abbreviated to NVLD. In my opinion, the name is very misleading. It is not very intuitive to square my masters degree in information technology and bachelor's degree in Philosophy, Politics and Economics with someone who is supposedly disordered in learning. After all, the word "disorder" suggests an impediment of some sort. Perhaps such a person cannot add numbers or read words.

But I certainly can do all that. I learnt later on that learning refers to the generic concept of the acquisition of knowledge. Acquisition of knowledge does not occur only in an academic context. It also occurs in other interactions with the environment. Maybe my condition should be renamed "Non-Verbal-Knowledge Acquisition Disorder". However, this wording doesn't solve the grammatical issue, which is where the word "acquisition" is placed.

The one handicap I do recall having was a speech handicap. I started speaking late, and had some problems pronouncing some words, so my parents sent me to a speech therapist for a few years. The speech therapist, whose name I can't remember now, was a friendly Aussie lady who possibly gave me sweets for pronouncing things correctly. Like my parents, she trained me using flashcards. I was reminded of that years later when I encountered Language Evaluators at Toastmasters correcting people's pronunciations.

My speech impediment didn't curb my hyperactivity, and I was always exasperating my parents by crawling fast in all directions. When I mastered speech and walking, I started telling stories in the sitting room. I would read in American storybooks later that kids had imaginary friends; I constructed an entire imaginary TV station with an audience of imaginary kids and imaginary parents in an imaginary country. My youthful pretend entrepreneurship alarmed my mother, who told me to stop talking to myself and write out the stories instead, lest people consider me as crazy in the future.

All this can be taken as further evidence that my verbal intelligence was very high. Even today I enjoy witty pieces, and have some appreciation of British wit. (In contrast, I find American wit to be either boring or sickeningly political.) Verbal intelligence is the component of intelligence that deals with words, language and concepts related to those. It also relates to the acquisition of grammar. I have had a fascination with languages for a long time. Being from Singapore, I am by default bilingual in English and Mandarin, but I am also capable of reading French and Spanish, and speaking/understanding some Japanese. I am definitely far from a genius polyglot, but my intelligence in this area is certainly not low.

I work as a software programmer in the daytime. I impressed my boss at probation by learning the programming language in one month, whereas it usually takes 4-5 months for other staff to pick up that programming language. To me, a programming language is just another language just like natural languages. In fact, programming languages are slightly easier because they are regular languages!

My issues are in non-verbal perception. While verbal intelligence has to do with "hard skills" like words and some aspects of mathematics, non-verbal intelligence has to do with spatial and social perception, the latter including what is known colloquially as "street smarts". One of the best illustrations of this would be an incident in my secondary school years. My family went to visit a darts bar. That is one of those places with dart boards and pool tables and people drinking late at night. Sometimes they may have a Karaoke booth too.

While my father was purchasing tickets for our family, I noticed a pool table that didn't have people around it. Basically, the people who rented the table had gone off to drink. That table also happened to have one unused cue stick leaning against a nearby pillar. I figured that since the players were not at the table, the table was available and I could just play a few shots. Plus, the table had a huge sign that said "first-come-first-serve". Since I came first, logically, I could use first while the other people were resting. I was puzzled when one of the guys came back and started scolding me for "stealing" their spot. I said, "What stealing? You weren't here, and I am not using your sticks at all." But my mother came over and apologized profusely for me. And afterwards, rebuked me for being "stupid". This was an example of a "social script" that I needed to learn, whereas to others it would be considered as "common sense".

A more humorous example occurred when I was in primary school. One day, I had a cold and sneezed in class. My kind teacher offered me a tissue. I was grateful to him for lending me the tissue. So I used the tissue, and then returned it to him. He was a little confused, and some of my classmates thought that it was funny too. That made me puzzled and confused, until he told me to throw the tissue paper away. In this case, the rule I was following was "return something that someone lends you", but I hadn't considered that it does not relate to dirty tissues.

Again, it would be appropriate to say that I lacked "common sense".

A much less humorous example occurred when I was in primary four, what some other countries refer to as fourth grade. I had been assigned with some of my classmates to do a project about our family trees. When we showed each other our family trees, I was curious about one of my classmate's ancestors, and so I pointed a finger at that particular ancestor's photograph. My classmate was extremely annoyed, because he thought that I was insulting his ancestor by pointing at the photograph. I don't remember the exact reason he gave for his fury, but I do remember what happened next. This classmate and the other one took hold of their staplers from their pencil cases, and started firing the staples at my legs, my shoulders and my face. That had so much effect on me, that to this day I will flinch if someone claps a stapler in front of me.

In fact, primary four was the worst year in my childhood. Various behaviours of mine irritated my classmates and my teachers, and as a result I was bullied horribly. Yes, by the *teachers* too. The teachers looked down on me partially because my mother chose to pack lunch for me. In Singapore, the typical culture is for students to buy lunch themselves from a student canteen. My first experience of a student cafeteria was when I studied my undergraduate degree in the United Kingdom.

However, many other reasons for bullying stemmed from other aspects of my non-verbal learning disorder. The music teacher mocked me because I had trouble tying my shoelaces, for instance. That has impacted me so much that I mostly stick to wearing shoes with velcro straps, except in the case of gym shoes, where I suppose Nike and Adidas and Reebok don't find velcro shoes to be "cool" enough or something.

In the end, my parents had to approach the Ministry of Education to get someone to talk to the teachers. After all, it was rather horrid that a teacher who was a pastoral counsellor started off a counselling session by asking the question, "what do you think you did that caused the bullying?"

Eventually, when I was secondary four and preparing for O-levels, my GP advised me to consult a specialist to see whether my coordination problems could qualify for an extension of time during my science practical exams. I was concerned that I might break test-tubes during the chemistry and biology practicals. That might potentially be dangerous. Not only did I obtain my time extension, but I was also diagnosed with Non-Verbal Learning Disorder, and that for me seemed to provide a kind of explanation for all my difficulties in life till then.

That being said, one positive result of that bullying was that it developed my interest in philosophy. That very unfortunate question my pastoral counsellor asked led me to a soul-searching of a sort, and this led me to a very arcane book in the bookshop: the *Meditations on First Philosophy* by the French philosopher Rene Descartes. I was intrigued by the topic of the First Meditation, about pretending that everything was imaginary. I decided to try that exercise for real.

Since I had difficulty in spatial perception, it was awkwardly comforting to imagine that space didn't exist. Although there were some instances where that was challenging to execute - like trying to imagine that your examination paper doesn't exist during an examination.

In any case, I preserved and grew my interest in philosophy. Despite the subject being about abstract concepts - which I am allegedly supposed to be poor at - it is a fantastically verbal subject as well; and that suits me to a tee.

However, we do live in a world where most people don't really think very philosophically most of the time, making it difficult to find a conversation partner, even on common interests. As an example, in university, I joined an interest group on Japanese animation. But what I preferred to discuss about anime wasn't really what others wanted to discuss about. The others approached it in terms of visuals and which characters shipped with other characters; and I was more interested in the assembly of the worlds and how Western culture was Japanized and other even more arcane topics. The manner in which I approached the topic was a totally different angle and path from everyone else.

Since primary school, I had lived with an acute sense of dis-belonging. Being in a university in a foreign country - even though it was one I had chosen - did give me lots of time to reflect on that. I joined the student boardgames society and found that I sort of belonged in that eclectic crowd, though not fully. Once after a role-play game at night, I joked with one of my co-players that I had a permanent degree of depression. Though afterwards I figured out that may be a half-truth.

Belonging is, after all, a key level in Maslow's famous Hierarchy of Self-Realization. There is a kind of existential grief or disappointment one feels in not being able to hit tiers of the Hierarchy. Most people feel un-fulfilled because they fail to cross the higher levels of Aestheticism and Self-Realization. As a neurodivergent, I fail to hit the lower level and so in a way the feeling of unfulfillment can be more acute than that of a typical.

Worse still, the world is becoming more complex. The new trend towards inclusivity of diversity is hell for someone who needs to acquire social scripts in order to function well in society. Traditional social scripts are already sufficiently complex; why the need to add in another thousand for "non-binary" identities. To me, all it does is add more mines to my invisible minefield.

In my case, it is really invisible. I do not even have hyper-sensitivities which can alert people as to my condition. Most people would probably treat me as just slightly disorderly or rude. I wonder if some of my behaviours would qualify me for an Anti-Social Behaviour Order in the United Kingdom.

I do not find myself personally humorous; perhaps the stress of figuring out social interactions is the cause of this deficit. But my inability to handle subtle social cues has rendered it difficult for me to appreciate or execute sarcasm. Like many people on the autism spectrum, I prefer direct and plain communication.

With all this in mind, when I thought of pursuing romantic relationships, I signed up with a dating agency. My rationale was so that I could be educated in the social scripts for dating, as well as spared from the need to analyze the various subtle cues of romantic interest and disinterest.

The match I picked was someone who was also neuro-atypical. I did so on the logic that an affinity in neuroatypicality would help us bond better. In the courtship stage, that seemed to work. But when we actually wedded, my hypothesis fell apart.

I surmise that this is because marriage - like many other social institutions - is constructed with neurotypicals in mind. Thus, even if two neuro-atypicals attempt to fit together in the institution, they will fail to do so, not because they are not compatible, but because both of them are not compatible with the institution. To abuse a metaphor, two square pegs can fit together, but they will not fit together in a round hole.

Where does that leave me, now? I don't really know. I guess time and God will tell.

Ze Shi's bio - Instagram @toxicat0m

Ze Shi, a 20-year-old aspiring fiction author on the autism spectrum, seeks to move and inspire others through his writing. In a compilation of stories, he aims to spread awareness and understanding about autism, lending his voice to the autistic community. With dedication and a commitment to making a positive impact, he advocates for acceptance and appreciation. Through his storytelling, he hopes to create a more inclusive world where every individual is seen, heard, and valued. Ze Shi stands as an inspiration for neurodiversity and the power of words.

Ze Shi contributed to our compilation because 'it's a writing opportunity' and 'Ever since I was diagnosed, I wanted to do my part and represent my community that I just joined. I wanna talk about autism with people'. He elaborates: Because I think that stories can change people. They can do a lot for people and I've read some amazing stories that did a lot for me. And I want to do that for other people. If one person feels touched, inspired, heard, listened (to), catharsis, wholesomeness from my writing... I can die a happy man. I just wanna inspire people with writing n like kinda express myself'.

Chapter Twelve

THE WRONG NOTE

By Ze Shi Soo

Imagine you are in an orchestra. Everyone plays their instruments on cue and the performance is going great, or so you thought. Though you played the notes perfectly and on cue as rehearsed, everyone is unhappy. The audience stops applauding, and the bandmates in your section cringe. *What happened*?

After the performance, you realise that somehow, you played every note wrong. Even though you followed the sheet music, even though you performed exactly like you rehearsed, and *no one* critiqued you then, somehow the same performance you delivered was suddenly wrong. And everyone pins the fault on you, and a week later, you are kicked out of the band.

That's what autism feels like. Specifically, being diagnosed after 17 years of cluelessness.

Autism Spectrum Disorder(ASD) is a neurodivergent condition that affects the person's socialisation and development due to differences in the brain, hence being neuro*divergent*. I was diagnosed at age 17 after my school counsellor noticed autistic traits in my behaviour, and having experiences with autistic clients herself, suspected I had autism. After my diagnosis, I was exempted from National Service and was given a Person With

Disabilities concession card that provided me discount benefits on public transport. Oddly enough, there was no history of autism in my family whatsoever.

The diagnosis did more than confirm my counsellor's hunch though, it also clarified doubts I always had when it came to socialisation. I've always struggled to socialise and create friendships that last, and never understood why until my diagnosis, and through many sessions with my counsellor, discovered huge holes in my knowledge when it came to understanding relationships. *I realised I was playing the wrong note this whole time.*

One lesson I learnt was that the moral of 'treat others the way you want to be treated', was incorrect, or more accurately, my interpretation of it was. For most people, the moral's message was that one should empathise with others' feelings and realise that their actions affect others, like how others' actions affect them. But for me, I understood the moral to be that *any* action or gesture which I would enjoy receiving, would be enjoyed by everyone else equally; *I understood it too literally.* And it was a huge 'eureka' moment when I realised my error. *So that's why it's a bad idea to lend my money to others carefreely.*
After more ground-breaking lessons, I began to worry. *What else have I been doing wrong all my life?* And I decided to play it safe, and muted myself. I became the loner again, and turned my own diagnosis against me. Other aspects of my behaviour were recontextualized, my leg shaking was actually a

stim(an involuntary movement used to regulate one's emotions, also known as fidgeting, *but more*), I *always* avoided eye contact, and I rigidly stuck to routines.

And then I grew spiteful. Seeing all the rules of socialisation before me, it felt like walking in a minefield while blindfolded. It's an uphill battle, and I always lose. Everyone was *Siris* and *Alexas* exchanging automated responses to each other, 'How are you?'. 'I'm fine.', 'This anime is so good.', all artificial fluff. I refused to participate in it, but had to otherwise I'd die of loneliness. I went back-and-forth, copying the stock replies but opening up at any chance I got, and in the end decided that those who followed the rules and those who expected others to, weren't worth the effort. *I'll play whatever note I want, and the whole orchestra can suck it.*

So I did, and avoided the shallow rule-lawyers, which was everyone. I ate lunch alone *vindictively*, I went home as soon as class was dismissed, *I* barely communicated with my groupmates, even when it was my Final-Year Project, and failed. And then I got kicked out of school afterwards. And I ended up lonely, *again*. The hole in my chest came back, *again*, and ate me up inside. I felt a thirst water couldn't quench, and desperately sought after it online. Any support group, any discord server, any meetup event, *anything, please?*

The more avoided, the more afraid I became, *what if I failed again?* I was already lonely, another rejection would be the final nail in the coffin, I can't afford it. No one understood me, because they've been socialising perfectly forever. It's so easy! Just be yourself, just have confidence, just don't be anxious, just learn social skills, just put yourself out there. *No one gets it.*

Not even the internet understood me. Just do CBT. Here are Ten Steps to Improve Your Social Skills! Step 1, *be yourself*, Step 2, *develop self-confidence*, Step 3, *manage your anxiety*, Step 4, *practise your social skills*, Step 5, *Practice makes perfect!* Where have I heard that before?

And then I got coaching services from a mental health start-up, HealthyGamerGG, #notsponsored. Every week, for 90 minutes, I met up with five random people and did my best to *talk*. It took me 16 weeks to do it, and another 16 to do it comfortably. *Step 5, Practice makes perfect!* How ironic.

And then I met Mark, from SG Geeks, a local group of, well, *geeks*. He read my story, which I posted online after mustering up all my courage, and *really* liked it, and wanted to meet up. Even though I didn't wanna go, I went anyway, and followed none of the rules, while feeling burning shame that I followed *none of the rules*. Yet, it turned out better than expected, and weeks later I got to have dinner with his friend and had a free ticket to Wakanda Forever. One of them, after the movie, asked me 'Who would win in a fight, Iron-man or Batman?'. Another rules-lawyer, another robot spitting out his 101 Icebreaker questions. This time, I followed the rules, and gave some stupid answer about Iron-man and his wealth, while keeping my genuine answer to myself: *That is not the point of these characters, you are superficially pitting them against each other and stripping them of their context and authorial intent, you voice-assistant stupid robot-*

And the dinner went well.

Wait, what? So I just have to follow the rules now? Be Siri? *Hey siri, the weather is hot today, don't you agree? Yes! The weather has been hot today, as it has been yesterday, and this whole week, and this whole month, and this whole year!* So I just have to fall in line, and be like everyone else? It was infuriating, but it worked, which was more infuriating! We met up to read comics, and I kept saying '*Oh wow, this comic is great!*', even though I was aggressively indifferent to them, and would rather read Dune on my phone. I had friends, at least. *So why am I Still Lonely?*

At least it was better than nothing, so I kept the act up. I tried opening up again, but only had a few strokes of luck. *You are wrong, Breaking Bad is the best television show, not Game of Thrones or whatever. Here are 101 reasons to support my argument.* And even worse, everyone was a working adult while I was a meek 17 year-old who knew nothing. I just kept silent while they talked about their work-life, and faded into the background until I heard my name. *And I wonder why I'm still lonely.*

I didn't belong there. I despised the majority of anime, I cared little for superheroes beyond a few TV programs, and *no one watches Breaking Bad!* I was too young, too inexperienced, too *different*, *what was I even doing in there?* And the hole came back, though smaller.

I enrolled in a private diploma, because I *needed* one, and was in yet another group of grown adults, even older this time. *I don't belong here...* The teacher grouped us together and gave us reflection questions to discuss, and they chatted about *stuff* again. And then it was my turn to share. Maybe it was because I was in a reflective mood, or the reflection question demanded a genuine answer of substance, but I answered honestly. A weight lifted off my chest, and the conversation *continued, and it was something I cared about; autism.* I told them how I got diagnosed, and how I struggled in polytechnic because of it, leading me to be kicked out and arriving here. *And I didn't feel lonely.* And all I did was follow-up on what they said with what I knew.

All I did was follow-up; *it was that simple.* And it worked like magic. On the MRT ride home, I learnt *another* ground-breaking lesson, the truth about socialising. It's just a game of follow-up. *You don't have to play the right note, you just have to continue the melody.* An answer, a comment, an observation, a recommendation, a story, an opinion, *a note*, anything works, it just has to follow-up. And that's how I played music, even though I hit the wrong note.

And wasn't that what I did, in the few strokes of luck I had when I did share about Breaking Bad? They said this show was the best, I disagreed, they asked why, and I gave 101 reasons why they were wrong. They didn't even watch the show, and still haven't, but I still got to have that conversation anyway, because I followed-up with it. I didn't follow *the rules*, I didn't walk on their eggshells, because *who cares* what actors they like, and I was unapologetically myself the entire way. And it worked.

I'll always play the wrong note. But I won't always create dissonance. And honestly, who cares about the orchestra? The point is to create music. Who cares about the relative strength of Iron-Man and Batman? Who cares about Singapore's weather? All that matters is Breaking bad, and who cares about the people who don't care about Breaking Bad? I'll just follow up everything you say with it and talk about it unapologetically. *And the orchestra can suck it.*

Interlude Seven

Day

By Arunditha Emmanuel

Day crept up from under the shadow of night,
said wake my slumbering child.
Take me in your arms,
kick the blanket off those dreams,
breathe in my light through your stirring eyelids,
pry your ears from that silencing pillow.
I wait unconfronted, my thirst for you unslaked,
come dance inside me child,
I'm ready for you now.

I'm sorry Day, I said.
My chest is hollowed out.
I need to fill myself with unsatisfied hope
and all the things that won't come out loud.
Leave me behind your blazing trail
so I can shiver in your wake,
draw the drapes after you,

there is only darkness here,
where time slithers on, a hungry snake
I just can't seem to feed.
I love you child, said Day to me
You're a promise for Tomorrow.
She asked I deliver you running wind speed
like to the forgiveness of your mother,
she'll smooth everything better.
Forget dried-out scale-skins of lost time
and things you cannot change,
I want you now and Tomorrow waits so
wrench yourself from this clinging bed,
untangle this debilitating sorrow,
it will form you a rope hard and strong,
to climb up conundrums and out black holes.

A noose won't keep me living,
I need you for that.
A noose won't keep me living.
I need you for that.
Okay Day, I said.
I'll start coming back.
Okay Day, I said.
I'll start coming back.

I'll start coming back.

Facebook:
https://www.facebook.com/deborahemmanuel88
Instagram: @arunditha.emmanuel
Website:
www.arunditha.com

Chapter Thirteen

Selective Mutism

By Carolyn Street-Johns
for Rennie Johns

When I, Carolyn, asked Rennie my husband aka
SpouseGrouse, to please do a chapter on his
condition there was unsurprisingly, pin drop silence.
As usual. I begged and pleaded. I reasoned and
bribed and I managed to elicit some dismissals. I got
the usual responses 'You do it lah'. 'I have nothing to
say' 'what I have is not good enough' 'what you
think doesn't matter, however much you say you
need my input.' 'Those were my thoughts whenever
my wife or anyone approached me for ideas, plans,
points of view, conversation on anything but

football!' - he revealed in conversation with someone

in a surprisingly articulate and other-centred response.

Sadly they are still all quotes that I hear frequently. As Rennie's wife of thirteen years I have noted them and have Rennie's permission to share here. 'You can read my mind, what!' is another one. 'You answer' he often says, when asked a question - however basic - in group settings. 'Carolyn can channel me' is another response. So I do my best and he nods, seeming relieved. I sigh, having hoped for any other answer in vain.

'I played alone as a kid because I didn't matter' is another snippet he has shared. When probed, there is nothing. Maybe 'I don't know'.

He has made some spectacular speeches, best of all was his proposal to me. We had been planning to get married since a few months into our relationship proper. It was always 'own time, own target'. But I asked him to propose when we were at my favourite spot once. It is a man-made (of course) cave feature with a waterfall at the front of it. It is in the Botanic Gardens here in Singapore. Contents private. I love spontaneous. 'I can't kneel down (because) it's wet' he said. I laughed, he shrugged and for once looked me in the eyes. I am not the fairytale nor swooning sort but it surpassed anything I could have dreamed of had I dreamt it as a 'normal' girl which I wasn't. Poetic, sincere, from the heart, utterly absorbing even for jaded public speaking trainer and head - of - Foreign - Languages - at -a - polytechnic - me. No less. Pure bliss, those moments. No embellishments for effect either from this reluctant teller of my story which should have been told by the person with experience of the condition known as 'selective mutism'.

It seems befitting to insert the story of our first meeting too. Our first meeting in real life (we met online) happened after nine months of texting and emailing as he was shy, was out of work and as he finally confided, lives with mild cerebral palsy. So mild one has to be very observant to spot it. But he would fall randomly as his motor skills didn't match his planned movements. Anyway we sat down in a Burger King of all places that evening the ninth of May 2009.

Over onion rings (I nearly called the date off when he asked for them, being a hater up to that point as I was. Instead I acquired the taste for them.) Where was I.. He spontaneously shared all about himself, his diagnosis by an eminent physician, he showed me his laminated copy of his exemption certificate from the standard mode of Military Service known as National Service or NS here. It is compulsory for all males post secondary education. He talked and talked and I relished it all. Lonely childhood noone wanted to let him play as he was different I guess.

Suddenly he said 'now your turn, you can speak too you know'. As the inside joke goes, I have not stopped. It is rare to have him entertain me like that. Rare to get a response that isn't 'I dunno' to questions like 'what shall we do today'. So when he does have a classic Rennie response to something, boy is it worth the wait.

Rennie qualified with me and two dear friends who we planned to go into practice with as a 5 PATH hypnotherapist and teacher of the 7th Path Self-hypnosis method, both by Cal Banyan. This was late 2017. I had become a Rapid Transformational Therapist and been to London for the live course with Marisa Peer herself. More on that topic in due course. So we were set.

He attended and got certified in Jin Shin Jyutsu®. Our key reason for getting married was a shared desire to cater to people with special physical needs. He dreamed of starting a gym and I caught that desire, being one with dyspraxia and the traumas of not understanding the rules and being the last person standing for teams. More on that in chapter eight. He caught on to my life's goal - to help folks with mental health issues of any and all kinds.

Rennie qualified with a diploma in Social Services with specialism in Disability Services. He was on fire.

Then - all gone. One job as a para-trainer gone. He had spoken out of turn. Another job gone; he had been oveooked for confirmation post-probation period. Let go after almost eighteen months as they could not justify having not confirmed him. Another job lost after a week - reason being he crumpled letterhead paper. Ask someone you know lacks fine motor skills to handle expensive paper out of the printer? Bananas.

All of this, every bit of it, I attribute to one incident that undid all the good work and faith-based and hard-won progress. Truth.

On Rennie's 50th birthday he started a speech he had planned. Backstory - he had joined Toastmasters begrudgingly with me in 2011, 6 months after we got married. Our shared goal was to date in a setting where we could meet people. My agenda was to get him out of his shell. A typical extrovert strategy with my 'adopted' introvert. And out of his shell he came, with lovely, encouraging friends from our own club and the various clubs we visited. He achieved the Advanced Communicator Bronze award. This was before our home club and the members who had come to know, value, encourage and love him - disbanded. Then he was retraumatised. This scene renewed my empathy for my spouse.

To continue.. The retraumatising episode happened at his 50th birthday celebration at his elder brother's home where his mum lives and where he lived till we got together, no less. 8th July 2018. He was delivering a special birthday speech and gearing up to a toast he had practised many times. It was a speech he had rehearsed at some Toastmasters meetings too. A good start, yay! He had everyone's attention and was mid-delivery. I was at the edge of the group checking he was audible and to be his encourager and stage-whisperer in case. I was really delighted. But the toast never happened…

Half way through was one of the punchlines which he had crafted. It was delivered with his tongue-in-cheek style and cute smile. Done better than ever. Rennie was on a roll.

For some reason his older cousin Augustine intervened. Augustine had had a few but not many drinks. He came out of the bathroom at that point. All eyes turned to Augustine who burped. Mid-speech. I had recognised him from snippets of Rennie's childhood stories. Like his two older brothers, Rennie the youngest, Auggie was someone Rennie respected and loved who had defended him when he was bullied at school and in the 'kampong' or village.

Then it happened. Without reading the room nor bothering to listen to Rennie at all, Auggie, the non-sibling confidant and role model he had always looked up to, came up to him from behind and put his arms around Rennie right there in front of family, friends, peers and the closest people to my husband. Mid-flow, Rennie looked round. 'Ah there you are, Auggie!' Rennie exclaimed

He was caught mid wonderful sentence. Flow gone. Augustine at that point chose to do that. He then said in my beloved orator's ear he said 'hush, hush it's all right, brother. No need, just have a seat. Chill! I will get you a beer. All good'. So used to following his beloved mentor and dear role model, Rennie did as Auggie said.

I was not close enough to start damage control. Abruptly he stopped, Rennie did. Everyone said 'yay good job' and 'wow' . All fake bravos. Like they really thought he had ended. But no. He had been stymied, cut off in his tracks. There is a great Malay phrase 'potong jalan', literally 'cut path'.

Of course Rennie hasn't attempted a speech since. And back into his shell he went.

I tried to get him to resume a bit later that evening but to no avail. He was sad. He had several rum and cokes in quick succession. 'Why?' He realised what Augustin had done. Music too loud, he fell back into wallflower mode as per usual at those family gatherings.

The Photo shows Rennie and Carolyn demonstrating Jin Shin Jyutsu. It is a hold that helps a person regain confidence and their authentic voice. Rennie is highly intuitive and an extremely gifted healer and he works as a coach and trainer for youth at risk.

Chapter Fourteen

Crystal Chapter

Crystals are some of our favourite things. Some are said to help with conditions like ADHD, ASD Dyslexia, and Dyspraxia, but it's not just about buying them and hoping for the best.

I (Carolyn) had very mystical grandmothers. As a kid in the 70s I picked up a lot from them. While a staunch Catholic, Mary my maternal Nan was into jade in a big way. She was Singaporean Indian and believed in its protection.

Jade Cross

I have no affinity for jade, personally except some of the lilac kinds. Nan, Albutha Mary Emmanuel her full name, always ensured I had a jade bangle on. When they broke she would have the jeweller reattach the pieces with gold.

Mary believed in food as medicine and had all sorts of remedies from Kerala such as indigo paste which she smeared on our cheeks when we had the mumps. she came to Singapore as a child.

We used to go to the beaches in and around the South West of

England and in Wales during the summers when we visited the UK to see my dad's family. Grandma and Grandpa lived in what was then the county of Hampshire. Gladys Grace, my dad's mum and I would search for stones with holes in them. She believed they gave off special vibes.

Let's talk about some specific crystals and what they're supposed to do. We have our own observations that support this list :)

Flourite Wand.

First up, we have Fluorite. This crystal is said to be an excellent learning aid, increasing concentration power and boosting self-confidence. Plus, it's supposed to absorb negative energy and encourage positivity. Natural Fluorite is actually colorless. The different colors come from impurities, and they can range from purple, lilac, golden-yellow, green, colorless, blue, pink, to champagne. Many types of fluorite even glow under ultraviolet light. They're "fluorescent."

Amber

amber is a natural gemstone formed out of pine tree and other resins up to 45 million years ago. Amber is great for anxiety and the worries that come with many conditions on the spectrum including ADD and ADHD especially. It helps with the embarrassment we often feel when our symptoms present themselves. It is also a great one for the sense of hearing, patience and a sprinkle of joy.

Muscovite

It is an excellent stone for you if you suffer from the symptoms of dyspraxia, including having problems with clumsiness and with left-right confusion. Muscovite will, as a bonus, help you if you have side effects from activation of psychic powers and psychic awakening, so we are told.

As we know one of the biggest tell-tale signs of ADHD is a 'so-called' lack of attention span. For folks who live with this, it can be a real challenge to stay focused or concentrate on just one thing at a time. Another symptom is "hyperactivity," where a person has a tough time sitting still. They might talk non-stop or be constantly fidgety. But fear not! There's a solution that can help keep impulsive thoughts and actions at bay, allowing folks with ADHD to concentrate on the task at hand.

We love amber, rose quartz, black tourmaline for these reasons.

Both attention deficit hyperactivity disorder (ADHD) and dyspraxia can prevent children from reaching their full potential in the classroom. While ADHD is a learning difficulty that often affects attention, behavior or both, dyspraxia has to do with fine motor skills, language and planning abilities and is not always classed as a learning difficulty. For us there wers no learning difficulties at all and we were often top in class. But having to wait for the other children was challenging.

Carolyn's awareness of her dyspraxia began at a young age. Unable to catch a ball leave alone take part in sports. This is aside from the 'exercise resistance that is a symptom of the pulmonary arterial hypertension. She was let go from a job at 7-eleven because she kept toppling the shelves. And cashiering was a joke □.

Another very useful aide is Sugilite. This crystal is said to help with Dyslexia and is supposed to enhance learning and problem-solving abilities. It's also said to be great for reducing stress and promoting inner peace.

https://thefifthelementlife.com/crystals-for-adhd/
Is a useful read

Carolyn has an odd kind of sort-of quasi dyslexia in which she confuses words with the same first sound. Quirky as ever.

Popcorn Calcite

Popcorn calcite, also known as Mexican onyx, is a beautiful and unique crystal that is believed to have powerful properties for boosting confidence. This crystal is known for its ability to help individuals release negative emotions and replace them with positive energy, which can help to improve self-esteem and self-worth. Popcorn calcite is also believed to have a calming effect on the mind and body, which can help to reduce stress and anxiety and promote feelings of inner peace and tranquility. Additionally, this crystal is said to enhance creativity and encourage a sense of playfulness and joy, further boosting confidence and overall well-being. Whether used during meditation, carried in a pocket, or placed in a special location in the home, popcorn calcite is a wonderful crystal for those seeking to boost their confidence and cultivate positive energy in their lives.

Add petrified wood, tiger's eye and rose quartz chrysoprase bible crystals black tourmaline rainbow tourmaline

Chrysoprase

I was drawn to this stone quite by 'chance' and fell in love with it. It fits perfectly in my palm.

It provides for non-judgmental attitudes and stimulates acceptance of oneself and others.

Chrysoprase is a strong detoxifying stone. It eliminates waste from the body.

Works on the mind as well, by stimulating the liver and encouraging the body to rid itself of poisons. It is excellent for relaxation and promoting a peaceful night's sleep, reducing claustrophobia and preventing nightmares.

Chrysoprase balances the hormones and treats the reproductive organs, fertility problems, and guards against sexually transmitted diseases. It treats disorders of the lungs and thymus, and soothes the digestive system. Aids mental and physical illness and exhaustion. Treats skin diseases and disorders of the heart. Chrysoprase increases the assimilation of Vitamin C.

Also Chrysoprase is known for promoting non-judgmental attitudes and stimulating acceptance of oneself and others.

If you're struggling with reproductive issues, Chrysoprase can help balance hormones and treat the reproductive organs, fertility problems, and guard against sexually transmitted diseases. It's also great for treating disorders of the lungs and thymus, soothing the digestive system, and aiding mental and physical exhaustion.

More about the fantastic benefits of Chrysoprase. This incredible stone is a total detox powerhouse, capable of eliminating waste from both the body and mind by stimulating the liver and encouraging the body to rid itself of poisons. Say goodbye to negative thoughts and hello to a healthier, more positive outlook on life!

If you're looking to relax and get a good night's sleep, Chrysoprase is the perfect companion. It's known for reducing claustrophobia and preventing nightmares, making it a great choice for those who struggle with sleep issues.

Chrysoprase is also great for balancing hormones and treating reproductive organs, fertility problems, and sexually transmitted diseases. It can even soothe the digestive system, treat disorders of the lungs and thymus, and aid in mental and physical exhaustion

Chrysoprase can also help treat skin diseases, disorders of the heart, and increase the assimilation of Vitamin C.

If all that wasn't amazing enough, Chrysoprase can even help treat skin diseases and disorders of the heart. So, if you're looking for a powerful stone that can help you on your journey to optimal health and wellness, the authors strongly recommend Chrysoprase.

But take note: crystals are not created equal. There are some fake ones out there that don't have the same properties as the real deal. So, it's important to know how to spot the real crystals from the fakes.

And don't forget about charging and cleansing your crystals. It's not a one-and-done kind of thing - you've got to keep up with it on a daily and monthly basis. But with a little intention setting, you'll be on your way to releasing negative energy and restoring your crystals to their original state.

Tiger's Eye ball

Another superstar for confidence is Tiger's Eye.
I love the blue one rather than the burnt-like orange one.

Black Tourmaline

Black tourmaline helps with steadiness and is a great pain reliever so it helps concentration. Black tourmaline is amazing for deflecting unhelpful energy (not necessarily negative; can be simply off-task energy)

True Story

Back in 2003 I was due to have surgery on my spine; lumbar 4 and 5 and coccyx. A thing called lordosis where the spine curves too far inwards concavely.

I was in extreme pain for months and was no longer the jumping bean as my students nicknamed me.

During a course on crystals one Sunday, after lunch we were sitting on the floor. I noticed my pain had gone. I had a look around the room, there was a black tourmaline on the floor a few inches behind me. It was not a huge stone but I asked Agnes Lau the teacher and she confirmed that the black tourmaline had helped 'fix' my pain.

Petrified Wood

Another favourite of mine for ADHD is petrified wood. For me it feels boring; the nesis state of ADHDers. I am more like the proverbial hare than the tortoise. The stone had at first such a slow, plodding, almost stuck vibe.

I was told it promotes patience and slow, steady progress. Petrified wood sounds startling (when a person is petrified, they freeze or 'stone' as we say in Singapore.

It helps so much with ADHD paralysis and overwhelm. Executive Function Disorder? Ah, all gone. It helps me with sequencing tasks rather than the stress and buzz of trying to multitask. Your modus operandi too? More haste, less speed is the message of petrified wood. Aye.

White Howlite

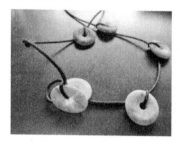

A wonderful stone for the hormones and the whole endocrine system. This necklace was specially made so the discs each sit on a Safety Energy Lock (from Jin Shin Jyutsu®)

I asked the authors of this and previous books what their favourite crystals for focus confidence and AD(H)D and the spectrum are:

Dianna loves Hematite

"Yep! Great for the circulation. (I) Breathe easier the moment I put it on. Pretty amazing" she says.

"Crystals are beautiful. But they shouldn't be used for superstitious purposes" said Clement

Christianity.com explains that crystals are considered occult because the Bible doesn't specifically mention their healing properties. Also because some use them to ward off evil and bring luck. So why are diamonds all right and clear quartz which is used to power so many gadgets? People use massage chairs and have massages with oil. The majority of medicaments in pharmacies and medications would be banned with that logic.

Annemarie from previous books picked Fuchsite

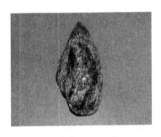

She has this important advice which is true in all cases.

"I have a beautiful piece of Fuchsite that is raw and sparkly. See the photo, courtesy of Annmarie Wilson. I tend not to pay any attention to the metaphysical properties as a lot of that is channeled information. I buy stones because I like how they look and feel. Historical information is interesting though - although historical is about as reliable as channeled.☐ Just choose what speaks to you ☐".

Fuchsite is a green crystal that is believed to have several benefits for individuals with ASD, ADHD, and confidence issues.

For individuals with ADHD and ASD, fuchsite is believed to help with focus and concentration. The crystal is said to help calm the mind, reduce anxiety, and promote emotional balance, which can be helpful for individuals with ADHD and ASD who struggle with emotional regulation.

Fuchsite is also said to promote self-confidence, self-worth, and self-love. It may help to release negative emotions and self-doubt, which can be a common struggle for individuals with ASD and confidence issues.

In addition to its benefits for focus and confidence, fuchsite is also believed to have physical healing properties. It is said to help with issues related to the immune system, respiratory system, and digestion.

Jireh picked Moldavite and Libyan Desert Glass.

Moldavite

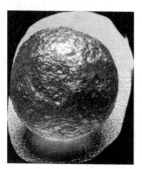

Moldavite is a rare, green-colored tektite, formed by a meteorite impact in central Europe. It is believed to have powerful transformative properties, helping to facilitate spiritual growth and enhance psychic abilities. In terms of confidence, moldavite is said to help individuals overcome fears and self-doubt, promoting a sense of inner strength and courage.

https://www.thelist.com/489155/everything-you-need-to-know-about-using-moldavite/

Says "Healing crystals also take center stage in our self-care journeys, with the demand for crystals and gemstones steadily increasing (via The Guardian). These stones are now used to project good energy onto their surroundings.." And "For those who are new to the world of crystals, the green stone probably shouldn't be your first purchase. That would be "like going to the Olympics before you've even run 100m," practicing witch Mariella Bucci tells Cosmopolitan. As a stone that has the energy vibrations to change your life completely, it comes with risks. It fundamentally depends on how you channel it, so it will go rogue if you do not give it any direction," Bucci continues"

Libyan Desert Glass

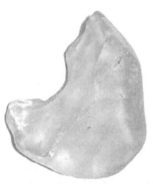

Libyan Desert Glass is a naturally occurring glass that is found in the Sahara Desert. It is believed to have a powerful energy that can help to stimulate the third eye chakra, which is associated with intuition, insight, and spiritual awareness. This can be helpful for individuals with ADHD or autism who may struggle with sensory processing or emotional regulation.

Jireh: "I got involved in crystals and the essential oils and stuff is due to me discovering the world of ritual and Magick"

" I like crystals and oils also cos of the multisensorial aspect"

"I discovered that due to the hypersystemisation of my psyche and sensitivity to symbol and archetypes, and the divergent way of thinking for systemises and forms connections v quickly I became very adept at crafting rituals based on need."

"I know all the elemental, astrological, alchemical, and also archetypal-mythological associations"

Crystals are amazing, learn to find out which ones are for you. The above info is purely subjective ☐

Interlude Eight

Shamanism

By Gudrun C Fritz

In Shamanism everything is spirit everything is here for a purpose, and brings harmony to the whole. There is no wrong or right, there are only universal laws to be followed to maintain the harmony between the beings on Earth. Now if we interrupt this system a shaman is called to restore balance

What kind of Shamanism do I do, asks Carolyn

I was trained in Classical Shamanism by Simon Buxton from the sacred trust. Afterwards, I continued my training with Michele Rozbitsky, in New Mexico. She is a pioneer in Native American shamanism and ceremonial. She taught me how the fundamentals have helped me to deepen my practise. Now I am in the process to find a new teacher, to improve and go beyond what I ever thought was possible.

www.gudruncfritz.com
https://www.facebook.com/gc.shine.5/

Interlude Nine

Anonymous

Prayer for the Lost

Dear Creator, Universe, Angels, Guides and our Highest Self

Do you mind enlightening me?

What is for my highest good and for my circle?

In this moment of time…

In this lifetime…

And for every period in between

Please guide me for I am lost and distracted.

Life is precious and the next moment is not guaranteed

In knowing that death is eminent, how may I best live?

How may I find my life purpose?

What shall I focus on in this moment?

What shall I focus on for my greatest contribution to the world?

How may I best serve the world with my multiple interests and talents?

How may I reap the best fulfillment and gains?

How may I best live in ways that lift my spirits?

How may I fill up my energy tanks?

Help me get organized, calm and joyfully productive!

Help me blast distractions, clutter and cumulative non-empowering things, people and events to the black holes.

Thank you for installing focus, discipline, goal & achievement programs in me.

Thank you for installing calm, restoration and rejuvenation programs in me.

Strengthen my will power and focus to be limitless ;)

Activate my abundance potential and my dream life

Say Prayer as many times as you like to activate it.

Bonus Interlude

By Stephanie Fam

Steph holding Cookie's hand   Steph Following Up

Glossary

1. Autism Spectrum Disorder (ASD): A developmental disorder characterized by challenges in social interaction, communication, and repetitive behaviors. It is a spectrum disorder, meaning individuals can experience a wide range of symptoms and abilities.

2. Attention Deficit Hyperactivity Disorder (ADHD): A neurodevelopmental disorder that affects a person's ability to pay attention, control impulses, and manage hyperactive behavior.

3. Aphantasia is *the inability to form mental images of objects (and events) that are not present."
"if counting sheep is an abstract concept, or you are unable to visualize the faces of loved ones, you could have aphantasiaAnxiety: A general term for feelings of unease, worry, or fear that can range from mild to severe and may impact daily functioning. And Generalized Anxiety Disorder (GAD): A chronic condition characterized by excessive and persistent worry or anxiety about various aspects of life, often without a specific trigger.

4. Avoidant Personality Disorder (AvPD): A personality disorder characterized by extreme social inhibition, feelings of inadequacy, and a strong fear of rejection or criticism. Individuals with AvPD often avoid social interactions and have a deep desire to be accepted and liked.

5. Asperger's syndrome, also known as Asperger's disorder, is a developmental disorder that is now considered a part of the autism spectrum disorder (ASD). It is characterized by difficulties in social

interaction, repetitive behaviors, and interests, as well as challenges with communication skills.

Here are some key features and characteristics of Asperger's syndrome:

5.1. Social interaction difficulties: Individuals with Asperger's syndrome often struggle with understanding and appropriately responding to social cues. They may have difficulty maintaining eye contact, understanding nonverbal communication, and engaging in reciprocal conversation.

5.2. Restricted interests and repetitive behaviors: People with Asperger's syndrome may develop intense and specific interests in certain topics or activities. They may also engage in repetitive behaviors, such as hand-flapping, rocking, or rigid adherence to routines.

5.3. Communication challenges: Individuals with Asperger's syndrome may have difficulty with the nuances of communication, including understanding sarcasm, humor, or non-literal language. They may have a tendency to take things literally or have a more formal style of speaking.

5.4. Sensory sensitivities: Many individuals with Asperger's syndrome are hypersensitive or hyposensitive to sensory information. They may have intense reactions to certain sounds, textures, or smells, or they may seek out sensory input to regulate their emotions.

5.5. Routine and predictability: People with Asperger's syndrome often prefer routine and predictability in their daily lives. Any changes to their established routines can cause distress and anxiety.

It is important to note that each person with Asperger's syndrome is unique, and the severity of symptoms can vary widely. With appropriate support and interventions, individuals with Asperger's syndrome can lead fulfilling lives and make significant contributions to society.

If you suspect that you or someone you know may have Asperger's syndrome or any other developmental disorder, it is recommended to seek a professional evaluation from a qualified healthcare provider or psychologist who specializes in ASD.

6. Bipolar Disorder: A mood disorder characterized by episodes of mania (elevated mood, high energy) and depression (low mood, loss of interest or pleasure).

7. Borderline Personality Disorder (BPD) is a mental health condition characterized by unstable patterns of emotions, relationships, and self-image. People with BPD may experience intense mood swings, have difficulties with self-identity and self-worth, and struggle with maintaining stable and healthy relationships.

Some common symptoms of BPD include:

7.1. Fear of abandonment: Individuals with BPD may have a strong fear of being abandoned or rejected by others, leading to desperate attempts to avoid real or perceived abandonment.

7.2. Unstable relationships: People with BPD often have tumultuous and unstable relationships, characterized by idealizing others one moment and devaluing them the next. This can result in intense and stormy interpersonal dynamics.

7.3. Impulsive behaviors: Individuals with BPD may engage in impulsive and risky behaviors, such as excessive spending, substance abuse, reckless driving, or self-harm. These actions are often driven by a need to alleviate emotional distress.

7.4. Emotional instability: People with BPD frequently experience intense and rapidly shifting emotions, including anger, sadness, anxiety, and irritability. These emotions can be triggered by seemingly minor events and may last for extended periods.

7.5. Distorted self-image: Individuals with BPD may struggle with a fluctuating and unstable sense of self. They may have a poor self-image, feelings of emptiness, and a lack of clarity about their goals, values, or identity.

7.6. Self-harm or suicidal behaviors: BPD is associated with a higher risk of self-harm, suicidal thoughts, or suicide attempts. These behaviors are often a desperate attempt to cope with overwhelming emotional pain.

It's important to note that BPD is a complex condition, and each person's experience may be unique. Treatment for BPD typically involves a combination of therapy, medication, and support from mental health professionals.

8. Dyslexia: A learning disorder that affects reading, spelling, and writing abilities, often due to difficulties with processing language.

9. Dyspraxia: A condition that affects motor coordination and planning, leading to challenges with activities such as handwriting, tying shoelaces, or coordinating movements.

10. Dyscalculia: A specific learning disorder that affects mathematical abilities, making it challenging to understand and manipulate numbers.

11. Echolalia: Echolalia is a language disorder characterized by the repetition or imitation of words or phrases spoken by others. It is commonly seen in individuals with autism spectrum disorders, but can also occur in other neurodivergent conditions. Echolalia can be immediate, where the person repeats words or phrases immediately after hearing them, or delayed, where the repetition occurs after a certain period of time.

12. Executive Functioning: The cognitive processes responsible for planning, organizing, prioritizing, initiating tasks, and regulating emotions and behavior.

13. Masking: The act of concealing one's neurodivergent traits or behaviors in order to fit in and conform to societal expectations, often leading to mental and emotional exhaustion.

14. Neurodivergent: This term refers to individuals whose neurological development and functioning differ from the typical population. It encompasses

various conditions such as autism, ADHD, dyslexia, and more.

15. Neurodiversity: The concept that neurological differences, such as those associated with autism, ADHD, and other conditions, should be recognized and respected as natural variations in human neurology, rather than being viewed solely as disorders or deficits.

16. Neurotypical: This term describes individuals whose neurological development and functioning align with the typical population.

17, Nonverbal Learning Disability (NVLD): A condition characterized by difficulties with nonverbal cues, spatial awareness, and visual-spatial processing, while often having strong verbal skills.

Object permanence
This refers to a person's ability to understand that objects continue to exist even when they are out of sight.
Babies are born withlut it. This cognitive milestone typically starts developing in infants around the age of eight to twelve months. Before this stage, babies believe that objects cease to exist when they are no longer visible. However, as their understanding grows, they begin to comprehend that objects still exist, even if they are temporarily hidden or removed from sight.

ADHD 'forgetfulness' is often due to this.

On the other hand, object immanence (impermanence) refers to the concept that an object exists independently of one's own perception or interaction with it. It is the idea that objects have their own existence and properties, regardless of whether or not we are interacting with them. So, even if we are not actively perceiving or engaging with an object, it still maintains its inherent characteristics and existence.

Both object permanence and object immanence are fascinating aspects of cognitive development, helping us understand how our perception and awareness of the world around us evolve over time.

18. Pathological Demand Avoidance (PDA): A profile within the autism spectrum characterized by an extreme avoidance of everyday demands and expectations. Individuals with PDA often exhibit high anxiety levels and may use avoidance strategies, such as distraction or negotiation, to resist demands.

19. Sensory Processing Disorder (SPD): A condition where individuals have difficulty processing and organizing sensory information from their environment, often leading to heightened sensitivity or under-responsiveness to sensory stimuli.

20. Stimming: Short for self-stimulatory behavior, it refers to repetitive movements, sounds, or actions that neurodivergent individuals engage in to regulate sensory input or express emotions.

21. Shutdown: A coping mechanism observed in some neurodivergent individuals that involves withdrawing from social interaction and external stimuli to restore emotional regulation.

22. Specific Language Impairment (SLI): A condition characterized by difficulties in acquiring language

skills, such as grammar, vocabulary, and understanding spoken or written language.

23. Schizophrenia: A chronic mental disorder characterized by abnormal thoughts, perceptions, and behaviors.

24. Tourette Syndrome (TS): A neurological disorder characterized by involuntary and repetitive movements or vocalizations called tics.

And this seems pertinent so for information: Dissociative Identity Disorder (DID)
        Interestingly, Dissociative Identity Disorder (DID) is not considered a form of neurodiversity. Neurodiversity refers to the concept that neurological differences, such as autism, ADHD, or dyslexia, should be recognized and respected as part of natural human diversity. It promotes the idea that these differences are not disorders or deficits, but rather unique variations of the human brain.
DID, on the other hand, is categorized as a dissociative disorder in the Diagnostic and Statistical Manual of Mental Disorders (DSM-5). It is characterized by significant distress and impairment in functioning, as well as the presence of multiple identities or personality states within an individual. It is considered a psychological disorder rather than a natural variation of neurology.

While neurodiversity advocates for acceptance and support of neurological differences, including those with conditions like autism or ADHD, it does not typically include conditions like DID within its scope.
        Dissociative Identity Disorder (DID), formerly known as Multiple Personality Disorder, is a complex psychological condition characterized by the presence of two or more distinct identities or

personality states within an individual. These identities may have their own unique behaviors, memories, and perceptions.

Here are some key points about Dissociative Identity Disorder:

1. Multiple identities: Individuals with DID may experience the presence of different identities or personalities, often referred to as alters. These alters can vary in age, gender, mannerisms, and even physical characteristics. Each alter may have its own distinct name, memories, and perceptions of the world.

2. Amnesia and memory gaps: Individuals with DID often experience memory gaps or amnesia for periods of time when a different alter is in control. They may not have any recollection of events that occurred during these periods, leading to confusion and disorientation.

3. Dissociation: Dissociation is a psychological defense mechanism that allows the mind to compartmentalize and separate traumatic experiences. In the case of DID, dissociation occurs as a way to cope with past trauma or abuse.

4. Coexistence of alters: The different identities or alters in a person with DID may coexist and interact with each other. Communication between alters can be internal (inside the mind) or external (through writing, drawing, or speaking).

5. Trauma history: DID is often associated with a history of severe trauma, typically occurring in childhood. This trauma could be physical, sexual, or

emotional abuse, as well as other forms of significant distress or neglect.

6. Interoception: According to Scholarpedia, Interoception is the sense of the body's internal physiological variables, their integration and interpretation. It is implicated in homeostasis and allostasis, as well as in emotional and self-related processes.

It is important to note that DID is a rare and complex disorder that requires a professional diagnosis from a qualified mental health professional. Treatment usually involves psychotherapy, specifically approaches like trauma-focused therapy and integration therapy, which aim to help individuals with DID integrate their different identities and work towards healing from past trauma.

If you or someone you know is experiencing symptoms that may be indicative of DID, it is recommended to seek professional help from a mental health provider who specializes in trauma-related disorders.

This piece partly deployed AI as ChatOn.

Dedications and Bouquets

My efforts in bringing Neurodiversity & Us about are dedicated firstly to my maternal Grandmother, my Nan, the late Albutha Mary Emmanuel the 17th of September 1919 - the 8th of August 1992.

She loved me and still does from above. As I mentioned in my contents she had me memorising poems and reciting them and I attribute my super memory of all things verbal to her. French and German vocab learning was a breeze. I can also recall clients' information without having to break rapport by checking dossiers or needing scripts for my Rapid Transformational Therapy sessions nor bespoke therapeutic audios.

The other main reason is that she loved, cherished and delighted in her fellow humans, of all shapes, sizes, creeds, younameit.

Her house, where I spent the best part of my childhood, was a haven for her myriad friends.

Growing up it seemed like she was entertaining or planning to entertain said friends, their families, their guests and she always had house guests which was a challenge for my mum, my three beloved aunts and three uncles. They had to do the cooking and we were always mingling, it seems.

She would accompany her friends to the Mosque, all sorts of Temples, and, being a dyed-in-the-wool Catholic, to churches not only Catholic ones but those of all denominations.

She is fondly remembered to this day by the members of 'The Kamala Club', a club for Indian women both Singaporean and not. As the story goes the clubhouse was reclaimed by the Government. Nan stepped up and her home became the official Clubhouse. Members held charitable events and hosted dignitaries from India. Their Deepavali gatherings are wonderful events to this day. Barely a handful remain from Nan's era but even those that arrived after she passed speak of her with love and a sense of honour for her. Mum, my Singapore- based aunt Priya and I represent her every couple of years, doing our 'part'.

Mary had an impressive lead crystal collection; not the natural crystals I love but hers sparked my keenness for the latter. I have mentioned her strong belief in Jade in the Crystals chapter.

Nan loved life. She spent her last years in a lovely suburb of Brisbane where she migrated to, to join my youngest and eldest aunts.

Nan and Grandpa Joseph had eight children, one of whom passed away as a toddler.
They were both school teachers who gave private tuition every spare hour they had.
She believed in education and sent five of her children overseas to study. Quite something in the 70s and 80s!
A traveloholic like me, she didn't get out of Singapore as much as she would have liked to. No doubt because Grandpa was a homebody; polar opposites the pair of them.

Grief & Us was dedicated to Grandpa.

Nan also loved to have Vedic astrologers round. My first name, which is Sanskrit, was chosen with their advice in mind.
Carolyn is my middle name and I love it too mainly because when people call me Caroline then ask which one it is, I smile and say 'Caroline is fine!'.
Here's to you, Nan with all my heart
Your V xxx

Bouquets

First and foremost to Snigdha aka Riley Bhowmik my large as life (virtual) Assistant. Virtual because we work virtually over zoom.

She does all the formatting, fitting things nearly into boxes, the layout as per Amazon's nitpicky instructions and . We have a lot of laughs and real conversations. I take care of the content, she brings it all to life.

Authors and interludes thanks for accepting the invitation. Thanks for the banter along the way and for all the help with my blind spots.

My school friend Tal asked key questions and helped me think ahead. With ADHD that help is a godsend. And for suggesting tangerine as our cover page colour. We initially had turquoise but that is for autism it seems.

Thanks Gali as ever, the inspired subtitle drafter. Thanks to everyone who chimed in with ideas.

Thanks Mum for believing in me and for all the love and support especially with this book.

Love Carolyn

Printed in Great Britain
by Amazon

25765076R00165